Love Letters

Love Letters

Eberhard Arnold

Emmy von Hollander

Plough Publishing House

Published by Plough Publishing House of
Church Communities Foundation, Rifton, NY 12471 USA
and by Church Communities UK
Robertsbridge, East Sussex TN32 5DR UK

The photographs in this book are from the archives of
Church Communities International

ISBN: 978-0-87486-939-2
11 10 09 08 07 1 2 3 4 5

Arnold, Eberhard, 1883–1935.
Love letters / Eberhard Arnold, Emmy von Hollander.
p. cm.
ISBN: 978-0-87486-939-2
1. Arnold, Eberhard, 1883–1935—Correspondence. 2. Hollander, Emmy von, 1884—Correspondence. 3. Love-letters—Germany—Halle an der Saale. 4. Courtship—Germany—Halle an der Saale. 5. Courtship—Religious aspects—Christianity. 6. Halle an der Saale (Germany)—Church history—20th century. I. Hollander, Emmy von, 1884– II. Title.
BX8141.A75 2007
289.7092'2—dc22

2007029393

Printed and bound in the UK by Athenaeum Press Ltd.,
Gateshead, Tyne & Wear

To Christoph and Verena
on the one hundredth anniversary
of the awakening in Halle

To the Reader

The complete engagement letters of Eberhard Arnold and Emmy von Hollander (nine hand-bound volumes of more than eight hundred letters) were first translated in 1968–69, and in 1974 a small selection appeared in the book *Seeking for the Kingdom of God.*

Selections for this anthology were made with an eye to conveying the most important aspects of Eberhard and Emmy's engagement, rather than reproducing historical documents, and were thus edited for style, clarity, and readability. In specific, archaic phrases were modernized, convoluted constructions simplified, and sentences (or whole paragraphs) abridged or omitted to avoid repetition and digression. Names of numerous "minor characters" (relatives, friends, and acquaintances mentioned in passing by the writers, but holding no special significance for the reader) were also removed.

Both Eberhard and Emmy cited numerous bible verses in their correspondence to inspire each other or to encourage further reading and searching on a particular issue. All but the most pertinent of these references have been omitted. Those citations left in the text have been supplemented with the actual verses in question.

A prolific poet, Eberhard penned dozens of verses for Emmy and often enclosed one or two poems when he wrote to her. In order to save space and avoid reprinting what is available elsewhere, almost all of these poems (and numerous references to them) were removed. To read them, see the book *Poems and Rhymed Prayers* (Plough, 2003).

Facts and anecdotes in the first chapter, as well as in the editorial interpolations throughout the book, were taken from Emmy von Hollander Arnold's "Locked Book" (an unpublished 1938 memoir); "The Story of Sannerz and the Bruderhof" (1931), also by Emmy Arnold; *Against the Wind* by Markus Baum; "His Way" (an essay by Eberhard's sister Clara Arnold); and other archival and family sources.

Contents

Background

"All of Halle is standing on its head," wrote the twenty-two-year-old nurse, referring to her hometown, where she was on vacation. "Wherever I go – to friends, to cafés, to social events – people are openly speaking about Jesus. The entire city is breathing a new spirit, and I yearn to be gripped by it as well. In many places you hear that this or that person has completely changed – even atheists and scoffers! Professors, military officers, businessmen, and students are equally inspired by the power of the message. People are literally dancing in the streets for joy."

It was the spring of 1907, and Halle, a bustling university town of 150,000 northwest of Leipzig, had come into boom times. At the close of the previous century, chemical and metal industries attracted by its location on the Saale River had put down roots, and now they were flourishing.

Seven short years before the outbreak of a war that would sweep this easy-going life away, it seemed that the good times would never end – at least for those in the city's wealthier neighborhoods. Yet even now something momentous was happening that would shake the comfortable lives of many. For some, the change would be forever.

Emmy von Hollander, the young letter-writer, was ensconced in Halle's patrician circles, with a family tree extending back centuries and replete with high-ranking civil servants and members of the Teutonic Order of Knights. And even if her father, a law professor, was stuck in an academic backwater that frustrated his ambitions, he clung to the lifestyle he felt his lineage demanded, maintaining a large town house and a troop of servants to care for his wife and their seven children.

To Emmy, the second oldest, the wave of exuberance she felt that spring in Halle was something new and unfamiliar. "God," she wrote, "was almost never talked about in our family. Certainly we went to church, but otherwise we found it embarrassing to speak about holy things." It wasn't that she didn't sense their power. As a child, she had lost a little brother,

The von Hollander children in Halle, 1901: Olga, Else, Monika, Gretchen, Heinz, and Emmy

and his death had made a deep impression on her. Later, as a teen, the confirmation classes she attended with her younger sister Else led her to dedicate her life to God, and drew her to nursing – not only as a profession, but as a calling. "I first worked with children in a hospital managed by Lutheran deaconesses. What moved me about the sisters I worked with was their devotion to God. Because of their influence, I gave away all my things, including my jewelry, to my brother and sisters." When her fourteen-year-old sister Gretchen died unexpectedly of appendicitis on the very pediatric ward where Emmy was working, it only deepened her dedication.

With the help of a family friend, Emmy found a second job in another deaconess-run hospital in Salzwedel in 1906. It was from there that she traveled to Halle in spring 1907 and found herself in the midst of a revival that had turned the city upside down. A certain Dr. Ludwig von Gerdtell, a brilliant orator, had just completed a series of public lectures on "The Living Christ."

Much of the movement took its energy from von Gerdtell's controversial emphasis on personal salvation and his boldness in attacking the institutional Christianity of the *Landeskirche,* or state church. Moreover, he was known to reject the doctrine of infant baptism in favor of adult baptism. But the "Halle awakening," as it is often called, was not limited to prayers and altar calls. It had practical consequences all over the city. In fact, according to Emmy's memoirs, it was "rare that a newly converted person did not have to give up his career." A well-known actor abandoned the theater for reasons of conscience. Eva von Thiele-Winkler, the daughter of a wealthy industrialist, renounced her life of privilege and founded a home for street urchins and orphans – a venture that inspired other similar ones across Germany. Suse Hungar, a teacher with a secure pension, gave up her job and savings and joined the Salvation Army, a step that impressed some but dumbfounded others.

In one way or another, thousands were changed by the revival. Naturally, plenty of people reacted with distaste, including Emmy's staunchly Lutheran parents. But for every churchgoer scandalized by von Gerdtell, there were others who responded with eagerness, among them Emmy's sisters, Else and Monika.

Soon the three of them were attending not only his lectures, but also the bible study evenings they inspired in the city's best homes, including that of Frau Baehr, the wife of a prominent surgeon. Thus it came about that Emmy was invited to attend an event in Frau Baehr's home on March 4, 1907, where a young theologian and friend of Dr. von Gerdtell named Eberhard Arnold was to speak.

> Else and Monika had no special desire to go, and my parents were not excited about it either. Going to a meeting in a strange house just wasn't done, unless there had been a formal visit to arrange it beforehand. I myself felt drawn by every fiber of my being, though at the same time I was a little nervous. But I finally went.
>
> We met in an impressive salon with an equally impressive mix of artists, doctors, and military officers' wives. Frau Baehr received me, and seated us all in a circle. Then Eberhard Arnold came in. After a short introduction, he

read Hebrews 10:19–23 and spoke with deep conviction on these words. The urgency with which he spoke struck all who were present, and we saw that it really is possible to have free access to Christ, to rid oneself of a bad conscience, to be washed in pure water. The whole circle felt this together; there was a common desire to experience the redemptive power of Christ, as expressed in the words, "Whoever looks in faith at Jesus on the cross is healed at the same moment."

Eberhard spoke with such power, with such fire and conviction, that afterward everyone crowded around him. The issue of truly experiencing Jesus' presence burned in us as never before. The movement had somehow laid hold of our hearts. I will never forget that evening.

Though merely twenty-four, Eberhard Arnold had long since dedicated his life to Christ. Born to a long and illustrious line of academics and theologians, he was the son of Carl Franklin Arnold (a respected professor of ecclesiastical history at the University of Breslau), and was the object of high hopes from early on. Indeed, his future seemed clearly mapped out for him.

Not surprisingly, young Eberhard chafed at playing his expected role, showing more interest in drinking contests and secret societies than good grades. At sixteen, however, a summer with an uncle changed his life. Ernst Ferdinand Klein was a rural pastor whose zeal for social justice had landed him in hot water more than a few times, and his passion opened his nephew's eyes to an entirely new definition of the Christian

The Arnolds in Breslau, 1902: Hermann, Clara, Elisabeth, Carl Franklin, Hannah, Betty, and Eberhard

life. Later the same year, in October 1899, a personal conversion altered Eberhard almost overnight and set him in a completely new direction. Soon he was throwing his energies into leading a bible study group of some fifty peers, evangelizing for the Salvation Army, and reaching out to alcoholics and homeless men in Breslau's poorest quarters – activities that disrupted his schoolwork to the degree that he only finished high school at twenty-one. Though his parents threw up their hands, his priorities were never a question to him: "I will never regret having worked for Jesus in caring for souls…It was his spirit that urged me to do it."

In 1905, Eberhard entered the University of Breslau studying (his father's idea) theology. He himself would have preferred medicine, but as it turned out, his stated field did not matter much, since what really occupied him was his involvement in the Student Christian Movement. Though hardly underprivileged, like the people he had previously sought out under the auspices of the Salvation Army, its members were earnest; and sensing a genuine awakening among them, he felt drawn to nurture it.

Eberhard eventually transferred to the University of Halle, but, as in Breslau, it was the SCM that filled his time and his thoughts – so much so that his fellow students elected him chairman of their chapter. Speaking at his inaugural address, he explained his goals:

> Honor to Jesus, our king, is what we want to represent. He alone is the firm rock of salvation for the anchorless wrecks that are tossed here and there by the opinions and tendencies of the present day. We place him in the center of a world that mocks him and says he is outdated. We do not want to be or become an isolated sect, but rather a missionizing power for all. We do not want to set up a party, but rather to unite Christians of every hue under the banner of Jesus...Only Jesus! That is the motto of our movement.

It was the Halle SCM that invited von Gerdtell to present a lecture series in late 1906 – the series that set off the revival Emmy met on her return to the city in early 1907 and led her to cross paths with Eberhard.

If Emmy was absorbed with the message of the young guest speaker that spring evening at Frau Baehr's, she herself did not go unnoticed by him. In fact, he had seen the fair-haired listener as soon as he entered the room, and told himself, "The girl I marry will be like that." Moreover, he felt such a strong premonition that this unknown young woman was to be his wife that he went to the Harz Mountains for a few days to try to clarify his thoughts on the matter and discern God's will concerning marriage. And God, he felt, unmistakably affirmed his feelings.

So it was that on their next encounter, March 24, at another evening meeting hosted by Frau Baehr, Eberhard could hardly contain his eagerness to exchange his first words with Emmy (a mutual acquaintance had meanwhile provided him with her name). He recounted this meeting for her in detail, in a letter written some time later:

> When I met you on the stairs, my heart was beating loudly. Though overjoyed, I said, with the appropriate reserve, "I am very glad indeed to see you here again." You gave me your hand and said, I believe, "So am I." You were so sweet, the way you looked at me, that I offered to take you home afterward, as you know. But you told me your brother Heinz was coming to get you.
>
> Then I ended up sitting in front of you, to one side. I felt your presence behind me throughout the meeting and was probably quite red-faced. It's amazing I was able to pass you without a mishap while helping with the furniture, because I was thinking solely about you. Later I waited for you at the door, and after we shook hands in silent farewell, I went

back to my room with great excitement. I kept walking back and forth and finally asked a friend (in strict confidence) how I should approach you in order to win your heart.

The next day, Monday, March 25, I went to Frau Baehr's in the afternoon with the thought of possibly opening my heart to her and asking her to invite you with me some time. That wasn't possible, since other people were there. But when Frau Baehr named those who were expected to attend the meeting that evening, and you were among them, I decided to stay.

Then came that important Tuesday, March 26, the day when, for the first time, we could have a real talk. I didn't accomplish much in the way of work. In the afternoon I was naturally at Frau Baehr's. Again I helped you on with your coat and was thrilled by your smile, which betrayed your happiness. Then I offered to walk you home, and though you thanked me, you declined. After this Frau Baehr drew me into a discussion, and you disappeared, leaving me in the lurch. I could barely suppress my fury at being stuck in an unnecessary conversation at an inopportune moment, but Jesus helped me to conquer.

In the evening I hurried to Dessauer Strasse, where, to my delight, I met you and your sister Olga. I saw that you were happy I had come to get you, even though you noted that we had not agreed on it. Olga was winning in her kindness, and I took it as encouragement. We spoke about the revival meetings and about my parents in Breslau. As soon as Olga was gone, I told you that I had heard you had decided to follow Jesus. You replied, "Yes, fully and completely." Then, as we walked along Friedrichstrasse, Wilhelmstrasse, Ludwig-Wucherer Strasse, and Dessauer Strasse, we spoke about the marvel of such a life, about witnessing to Jesus, about Salzwedel, my conversion, our families, etc. We were both so happy and full of trust.

Then I went to the wall opposite your house, prayed long and earnestly on my knees, and finally received from the Lord the certainty that you would become mine. After this I went into a café on Geist Strasse and had something to eat. From there I went out on the heath, where I experienced the most glorious night of my life, praying and thinking of you.

Wednesday afternoon I went to Frau Baehr's again, where I found you sitting at the grand piano. Later, on the way to your house, we got onto the topic of Salzwedel, the importance of testifying to Jesus there, the difficulty of your situation at work, and your loneliness there. I felt that letters could help, and on the way home I asked you whether we might correspond. You thought that would be very nice, but that it wouldn't work on account of the rules at the hospital. I insisted that we must find a way. We then agreed to correspond via your parents.

Arriving at your door, we took each other's hand and agreed that we belonged together. And so, after three times twelve hours, we were betrothed forever.

Happy as Eberhard was in Halle – a young man in love, in spring – circumstances dictated that he return to the University of Breslau, an eight-hour journey by train, to continue his studies. A new semester was to begin right after Easter and, as he wanted to spend the weekend with his parents, there was little time to meet Emmy's parents, gain their approval, and proceed with a formal engagement. Taking the matter in both hands, he told Emmy he would visit her family in two days, on Good Friday. She did not know what to expect:

> On Good Friday, in the morning, my sisters and I went to the cemetery near our house, where our fourteen-year-old sister Gretchen and several acquaintances were buried. On our way home we saw Eberhard ahead of us, dressed in a formal black suit and coat, with a top hat. He was carrying flowers in white paper. We entered the house behind him and sat down in the dining room. He was already talking with my father, and I heard my father saying, "I have heard that you would like to correspond with my daughter."
>
> "Yes," said Eberhard, "But not only that. I would like to be engaged to her – today."
>
> "That's out of the question," my father replied. "She tells me you have lived a clean life, that's true, but I don't even know your parents' position."
>
> Eberhard answered, "My parents trust me to choose the one meant for me by God." After saying this, Eberhard asked to have a private conversation with me. My parents consented.
>
> When we were alone, Eberhard told me that God had given him the conviction that we belonged together for life. I answered that the same conviction had come to me,

and we were engaged. Then Eberhard took a Bible from his pocket and we read the thirty-fourth Psalm together: "I will praise the Lord at all times." Then we prayed together, placing our lives in the hands of God and promising to serve him and witness to him forever.

Afterward, my parents and the rest of the family came in. My brother and sisters immediately accepted their new brother-to-be, but my parents said they would only agree to our engagement when they had heard from Eberhard's parents. Then Eberhard went out into the corridor and brought back a bouquet of dark red long-stemmed roses for me and white roses for my mother.

He came back to our house in the evening and again at midday the next day. We were alone part of the time, and partly with my brother and sisters. On Saturday he left for Breslau. I was allowed to accompany him to the station, but only in a closed cab as my parents insisted we keep the engagement secret until Eberhard completed his studies. On Easter Monday I received my first letter from him.

Jesus!

First Love

En route to Breslau
March 30, 1907

Always Philippians 4:4: "Rejoice in the Lord always. I will say it again: Rejoice!"

Ephesians 1:13–14: "And you also were included in Christ when you heard the word of truth, the gospel of your salvation. Having believed, you were marked in him with a seal, the promised Holy Spirit, who is a deposit guaranteeing our inheritance until the redemption of those who are God's possession – to the praise of his glory."

My Emmy,

How poor are words in conveying the heights of splendor as I would like to! Yet how rich are our hearts that they can feel – no, more, experience – these splendors!

How wonderful it is that even in the most contradictory surroundings we can hold fast to this precious treasure in its fullness! And how glorious that two people like us are able, despite the poverty of speech and despite all other obstacles, to share it fully with one another!

My sweet little darling! On this rattling train, among people whose aura could not contrast more with that of the last days, I am reflecting on the glorious grace God has poured over us, and rejoicing in the invigorating memory of our unforgettable time together and our unclouded happiness. Your sweet photographs give me special joy. If only I could be with you and tell you and show you how endlessly I love you!

Longing for you joyfully in Jesus,
your Eberhard

Excuse the appearance of this letter. It comes from the jolting of the train and my shortage of writing paper. But I couldn't help writing at least this to you. The rose is keeping beautifully. 1000 kisses! Greet everyone warmly!

Emmy also put pen to paper not long after their first parting – and thus began a flurry of letters that would continue for almost three years. Breslau might be hours away, but corresponding was easy: thanks to the efficient German postal system, letters mailed from a train station generally arrived within a day, even on weekends. Besides, Eberhard's close acquaintance with the leaders of the Halle revival, and Emmy's own intense involvement in it, gave them both plenty to tell each other. (Lucia Franke, a young woman mentioned in the first letters, was a mutual friend who was romantically inclined toward Eberhard.) But beyond such news, both wanted much more – a relationship based on discovering what it means to follow Jesus. These would be no ordinary love letters.

Halle
March 30, 1907

My beloved Ebbo,

Just now (it is 5:30) as I sat down to write to you, it occurred to me that I don't even have your address! But then Olga had the clever idea of ordering the Breslau address book, which I plan to go pick up myself right away.

You know, I keep thinking of what you might be doing now and whether you are thinking of me. I keep looking at your picture, the roses, and the sweet ring, and missing you dreadfully. That probably sounds awful. I really shouldn't complain – rather, we ought to be thankful that God our Lord has led us together so wonderfully. I just keep wondering whether you will find enough substance in me, since you are much farther along than I am in the knowledge of our Savior and of the Bible. Of course, this is exactly what you must help me with, and that's what you want to do.

Not long after you left, Olga and I went out for a walk. We met Lucia Franke. I greeted her very warmly – I felt you would have wanted me to – and she returned my greeting.

A few times I stopped, thinking I saw you, but each time I was bitterly disappointed. Oh, how lovely it will be when you are here again! I am so happy thinking about it.

This evening I am going to read the last two little volumes you gave me. I love how you always place Jesus firmly in the center. I wanted to talk about it with you earlier today, but there wasn't time. There was also something I wanted to ask you about von Gerdtell's lectures. But that would take too long, and then my letter wouldn't reach you tomorrow – at least that's what I'm afraid of. So I'd better close. There is so much more I could tell you. But I'd better leave it until tomorrow. Greet your family very warmly from me and tell them we are both terribly happy.

United forever in our Lord and Savior,
your warmly loving Emmy

This letter is confused, but I know you'll excuse it and understand.

Breslau
March 30, 1907

My sweet, beloved Emmy,

I just can't describe how happy I am! My parents congratulated me with extra warmth when I got back, and found your photos totally captivating.

My sisters, Betty, Clara, and Hannah, are giddy with happiness. Another time I will write down their questions for you, and everything else. For now, everything is so glorious, so glorious, my only love, my darling Emmy! Really, things couldn't have come about more wonderfully!

Unfortunately, no one could meet me at the station, since my dear mother had a bad attack of pain from her gallstones. When I arrived, however, she was quite all right and exceedingly happy about my news. She is in bed now, but still wants to write you a few lines, full of her love, I am sure.

Papa is going to write to your father tomorrow, so he ought to receive a letter on Monday morning. But I must stop now, otherwise this letter won't make the train. How indescribably glorious that you are mine, that I am yours, and that we both belong to the Lord, and all this completely!

In deep, unending love,
your faithful Eberhard

Breslau
Easter Sunday, March 31, 1907

"His possession for the praise of his glory!"

My beloved Emmy,

This morning the mailman must have had an unusual amount to do, and I ended up running back and forth from the balcony to the window to the front door for nearly an hour to see whether he was finally coming. And then it suddenly occurred to me, too, that you might not have my address! What a scare – I thought of how awkward it would be for you and was about to send you a telegram. But then at long last the letter I was waiting for so fervently arrived, making me so terribly happy.

How magnificent that you can write: "I do not want to complain..." "We have much to be thankful for!" "I am too happy..." "United forever in our Lord and Savior!" Every word of your sweet letter is worth so infinitely much to me! I also miss you terribly, you delightful, darling little person!

My sisters are amazed at how much we were able to share in so few hours, and it's true that we have already told each other a lot! Oh, I wish I could hold fast forever to every word, every look, every kiss of those marvelous hours on March 29 and 30! Yet I have more: I have *you* forever! Oh, my happiness cannot be imagined, much less expressed!

But wait – so many things keep occurring to me that we must still talk over, that what we have discussed so far is very little by comparison. I always want to tell you everything, *everything* that I'm thinking and learning and experiencing.

I am so happy that my picture, the roses, and the ring give you such joy. I am writing at my desk – a handsome little mahogany piece that belongs to me – and on it I have arranged your pictures, which are amazingly beautiful. In the center I have placed a small, snow-white alabaster cross. You know, it is not without significance that God arranged for our betrothal to take place on Good Friday. Our engagement and our entire life must be lived completely under the sign of the cross, the cross that has brought us into such a glorious relationship with God, as his children. The cross has obliterated our sins and revealed the highest love of our God and Jesus, and it has the power to let us die to sin and the world, so that we can live for him! I am attaching the rose you pinned on me in farewell to this cross.

How often have you kissed your ring? I can't count the times I have kissed mine! My sisters advised me to put on a second ring as well, so that people will not ask me whether I am engaged. What do you think? Shall we both do this?

My beloved bride, not only will I have enough in you, but I'll have much more. You are, apart from the redemption Jesus offers, God's richest, most inconceivable gift to me, one that I will never be able to fathom or to exhaust. The very thought of having such a bride (I'll avoid going into detail, for we don't want to make each other vain) strengthens me; it is an incentive to serve my Jesus more fully and purely.

As for your Christian understanding, it will grow in proportion to the increase of your joyful determination to serve him alone. Pray in all questions with a simple, childlike trust, and he will give you his answers ever more clearly. And study your Bible with eagerness and devotion. What do you think – shall we both read the same chapter every day? Then we can always speak and write about it. Would you rather start with one of the Gospels, or a Letter? What would you think of Matthew? Or what do you suggest?

Incidentally, I plan to send you a good book from time to time.

Thank you for greeting Lucia Franke with such kindness. I'm enclosing a letter to her, which I've discussed with Clara, and I'll send it off this evening. Please tell me exactly what you think of it.

I'm so glad that you, too, love to see Jesus always in the center. That alone is healthy Christianity. Not doctrine, but Jesus. Not emotions, but Jesus. Not efforts, but Jesus. Always, nothing but his will, his peace, and his power!

I'm very eager to know what you want to ask me about von Gerdtell's lectures. Write down everything for me – it can never be enough. And I don't find your letter confused at all. That's the marvelous thing: that we don't write with cool, analytical logic, but with our heart's blood. Certainly logic, order, and objectivity can go hand in hand with the enthusiasm of love, but only where possible. Until we meet next, shall we write to each other every day, my sweet Emmy? After that, however, we must put a tight rein on ourselves so as to make the most of our time and fulfill our obligations.

My sisters (my brother is with his fiancée, Käthe, in Schweidnitz) are so pleased about us. Today at noon we all made a toast to you, with white wine – even Mama, though she was quite unwell. And later, on a wonderful walk with Papa, during which he had me tell him all about you, he said something that made me very happy: that he, too, sees our engagement as God-given. He asked me so many questions about your family that what I knew wasn't enough for him. He was glad that we are happy, but also gave me some important things to think about. Above all, he insisted that I must put all my energies toward being able to provide a secure livelihood for ourselves as soon as possible. Certainly, I do not draw the same conclusion as he does from this – that I should be aiming for a position with a pension, such as a parish. I am certain that my Lord will take good care of me and mine, if I go his way joyfully, as far as I see it, even if it seems outwardly disadvantageous. And this is exactly what you feel, too, my Emmy, isn't it?

Additionally, my father would have liked to know more about your parents' families. Please tell me about them, and also explain why the crown on your stationery has seven points instead of five.

On the first evening, when everyone was asking about you, it was amusing that one of the first questions was whether you were of the nobility, and whether your father was a professor. Afterward there was so much talking and rejoicing that I can't possibly write it all down. Betty then sang several beautiful love songs for me.

Papa just showed me a very nice letter he wrote to your dear father, to finalize our engagement. Oh, let us jubilantly thank, thank, and again thank our glorious God for his unending grace!

Now it's high time I went to the station to send off this mail. So here are just a few requests:

1. Please send me one of your beloved curls, but not so that it spoils your hair.
2. If possible, have yourself photographed (unless you've already done this) in two poses: one full-face, and one more in profile. I am sure you'll think of me while being photographed and will look happy and natural.
3. Give your – no, *our* – beloved parents and brother and sisters my warmest greetings, also from my mother, who has been feeling better today; and tell dear Olga that her little book has been very useful.
4. Please ask if I might come on the 13th or 14th. I'd like to arrive early, if the Lord allows, and to bring Betty along. She happens to be traveling to Bremen.
5. Above all, let Jesus occupy the first place at every moment,

and place everything under him, in particular our relationship. Test everything, pray about everything, and tell me everything! As I whispered into your ear yesterday: I am yours, you mine, and we are his!

In deepest love,
your happy Ebbo

Always be joyful! We'll see each other soon! Of course, write me with any wish. It will make me happy to fulfill it.

Raised according to the time-honored code of Germany's nobility, the von Hollander daughters were conscious of their family's place in the world, but dissatisfied with it. Emmy, in particular, chafed at both the privileges and the obligations her class conferred on her: "I did not want to be just another daughter in another genteel family." Already as a child, she was upset that certain girls in her school could not afford confirmation dresses; and later, though the family's maids left her and her sisters ample opportunities for the sedate, cultured activities young women like them were expected to pursue, she spent her time serving others. Even on days off from her job as a nurse, she visited elderly and sick acquaintances.

By the spring of 1907, as the Halle revival reached its climax, Emmy was attending bible studies and prayer meetings almost daily and eagerly reading the pamphlets distributed by its leaders, especially the booklet, "Advice for the Newly Awakened." And at every opportunity she was reading the Bible as if discovering it for the first time.

Halle
April 1, 1907

My beloved Eberhard,

You can't imagine how glad I was to get your letters – the one you wrote on the train and the long one from Easter Sunday. Both of them made me inexpressibly happy. And it was very kind of your father to write so warmly to mine. Papa and Mama are just now writing in reply.

Of course you should come on the 13th and bring Betty with you. We would be thrilled if she were to stay with us a few days. Unfortunately we won't be able to offer her lodging here, since we have no guest room at the moment. I'm already using the small living room as a bedroom. But a close friend of mine – the woman we confided in regarding our engagement – wants me to invite Betty to stay with her. She has a very large house with a lovely guest room, and lives alone with her mother, so there won't be anything conspicuous about it.

O Eberhard, I am so inexpressibly happy that I now have someone in whom I can confide *everything.* My happiness is unimaginable! I keep looking at my ring, and can't count how often I've kissed it. You know, I think it would be nice if we wore only our engagement rings – though if your sisters think people will notice, it might be better to wear another one as well, after all.

What a fine thought that both of us should read the same bible passage each day! Then I can ask you about everything I read. I think I'd rather start with one of the Gospels. Matthew would suit, or John. But tell me the one *you* would rather begin with.

I wanted to ask you something about the Lord's Supper. Von Gerdtell says it is merely a meal of fellowship and remembrance. He claims the Bible says nothing about forgiveness of sins. But then why does Paul say that whoever takes it unworthily eats and drinks judgment on himself, and why did Jesus, when he instituted the Lord's Supper, say it is "for the forgiveness of sins"?

By the way, I think your letter to Lucia is very good. You wrote very kindly, and yet she will be able to infer from it what she is supposed to infer. I think we can now let the matter drop.

About your position – whether you should become a minister or a missionary or something else – I cannot advise you. I can only say, "Where you go, there will I go; where you stay, there will I stay. Your people are my people; your God is my God. Where you die, there will I also die, and there will I be buried."

Unfortunately I must close. I still have so much to tell you about my family, especially Else and Monika. But this letter has got to go now, or else you won't get it tomorrow morning. I will have my photo taken as soon as I am no longer so pale – Mama says I should still wait a couple of days. I also am going to write to your sisters – I was so pleased to get their letters.

Your extremely happy Emmy

Halle
April 3, 1907

My dearest beloved Eberhard,

Yesterday, just after I gave Heinz the parcel to mail, I got the letter from you that I was longing for, which made me very happy. (Incidentally, I was at the photographer's today.)

Last night I was invited to Frau Baehr's. We had a glass of wine, and she was so charming. She kissed me over and over and said it was now clear to her that our engagement is God's will – that we belong together. She even wept for joy. She said that on Good Friday she had asked God for clarity, and that he had answered her with the words from Jeremiah 32:41–42: "I will rejoice in doing them good…" I had to tell her all about our engagement (naturally only as much as can be told), and she was especially happy that we prayed together. She is also going to help me meet the Christians you mentioned. She said that a lone cornstalk breaks too easily. She then advised me not to return to Salzwedel too quickly. She says I should first deepen myself in Jesus, in quiet. Besides, my parents would prefer for me not to commit to going there before July 1. Because of this, the timing of my trip to Breslau is no longer as pressing as it was – it doesn't have to be before the Whitsun holiday. Of course, what I'd really like most would be to travel as soon as possible so I can get to know your dear parents and sisters and brother.

The delightful roses you gave me for our engagement are in front of me, and still beautiful. I look at them constantly; they make me so happy. By the way, when being photographed, I held my hand in such a way that you can see my ring. I hope you like the way the pictures turn out. Are the violets from your garden?

Emmy, 1907

I wanted to write to you about your articles – actually, I would rather talk to you about them in person. The thought I liked best was this: "God wants all people to be helped: this means a personal decision either *for* Christ or *against* Christ." Most people tend toward a half-hearted decision, which is a terrible thing. I also think it is better to have no Christ than half a Christ. Another sentence that jumped out at me was:

"We believe that the power of the blood of Jesus Christ, of his dying and living, can show itself powerfully even in youth, during one's student days. We believe that young men and women can find their greatest fulfillment through giving themselves over to Jesus in trust and obedience." This sentence made plenty of sense to me, especially since I had formerly thought that Christianity lacked real power; I guess I believed in a Christianity based on feelings. To me, the way you describe conversion makes it all so simple and clear.

There is just one thing I can't quite understand. You write: "Young people are inclined most of all to put their inner feelings in place of the obedience of faith." I thought this was basically the same thing – surely, the obedience of faith comes out of an inner feeling. God usually speaks to us through an inner feeling, and if one listens to that, I call that the obedience of faith. I don't mean by this that there can't be obedience of faith *without* inner feeling. But it isn't wholly clear to me.

Tomorrow I will write more. Today Else and I have been invited to a woman who used to be our teacher. So I have to bring this to a close. I just received your letter. The poem made me terribly happy, and the texts also moved me very much. More tomorrow. My mother just came in and is moved by your letter.

A thousand greetings,
your warmly and endlessly loving Emmy

Breslau
April 6, 1907

My beloved Emmy,

It's impossible to say how happy it always makes me when your letters arrive. And how punctually they come! I'm ashamed I haven't always managed that. Today there were even two! You know, I read your letters over and over. Even if later we can't correspond as often, we will always have the letters from these wonderful, rich, first weeks. It is splendid that we can tell each other *everything* – the deep, the beautiful, and the marvelous, but also the difficult and sad things. And we can be grateful there are so few sad things to tell each other, and so many infinitely joyful ones.

Dear Emmy, faith does not depend on feelings. It is not feelings but the *will* that forms the character, especially the Christian character. Often we must continue on the way simply through strict obedience, quite soberly, while at other times the Lord will overwhelm us with floods of joy. He does both in order to teach us. The peace of God is *not* a feeling. It is the relationship of the soul to God, and an expression of the fact that a reborn person is a child of God.

Jesus' baptism in Matthew 3 is, I believe, the first moment in his life that brings his vicarious role clearly to the fore. He became man in order to redeem man, as a Savior and sufferer. As a human who thus bore humanity's sin – though he himself was sinless – he subjected himself to death for the forgiveness of sins and in order to fulfill the demands of justice. By the way, it is wonderful that on Sunday we will read Matthew 5. It is so deep.

The book *The Court Preacher* gives me great pleasure. However, I find our own love story even more wonderful. By God's grace, the meaning of full surrender to Jesus is even clearer to us. It's also wonderful that we didn't have to wait so long to find each other. I doubt you could find another such example. O my sweet, beloved bride!

Today I was with Georg Herde at the Oder, and watched a purple-gold sunset over the water, and thought constantly of you and of the fact that you might be here very soon, enjoying everything with us. I'm glad the roses have kept so well.

All right then – until the evening of the 13th in Halle!

Endlessly happy in Jesus and in you,
your loyal Ebbo

I will get a copy of the "Glory Song" for you. And greetings from my family!

Halle
April 9, 1907

My beloved Eberhard,

Today you again made me tremendously happy with your loving letter and the songs. Monika and I already sang the "Glory Song" together. Thank you so much for sending it. I haven't yet read the other writings. I skimmed your article in the *SCM News,* and will read it again; the same goes for the other two writings. I am so sorry you had to wait for my letter yesterday. I hope the one I sent today won't be delayed. Both were mailed by 8:30.

You know, I'm very unhappy today. I think I was too zealous yesterday. I said it wasn't right for a Christian to have an active social life, and stated my view quite bluntly. Mama was very angry and said I was one-sided. It definitely would have been better for me to say nothing, as nothing was gained by it. After all, it doesn't apply to me any more, because of our engagement, and it is surely none of my business if others go out with a good conscience. In any case, I will be more careful. Besides, I believe that a busy social life is more of an occasion for sin for some people than for others. (I am speaking only of Christians, of course, since for worldly people I don't think it's an issue at all.) What do you think?

In Matthew 7:7–12 it says that God will give you *everything* you pray for in faith. Yesterday my sisters and I were talking, and I quoted the passage, "If you had faith, you could move mountains." At this, Olga said she understood these words differently; otherwise I should (for example) pray that you'd be finished with your studies in a week. What do you think? Frau Baehr explained her view on this by quoting Matthew 7:13–15: "Enter through the narrow gate." But what about verses 15–23? Please write.

This afternoon I am going to visit two old ladies, one of whom is ill. It will be rather difficult to be open and still remain quiet about our engagement, because they are very curious. Frau Dr. Schulze, by the way, asked me yesterday whether you were still in Halle. I just answered "No," and then changed the subject.

I'll have to throw out the roses today – they don't look very nice anymore.

I'm looking forward like anything to Saturday evening. It's only four more days now, and then you'll be with me, my beloved!

In deepest love,
your loyal and happy Emmy

Breslau
April 10, 1907

My dear, sweet Emmy,

How I look forward to seeing you the day after tomorrow and to discussing everything with you! You know, last night I got really sad – I was also very tired, of course – realizing how unworthy I am of you. I have to be honest: the thought came to me that you are going to be very disappointed in me, in many ways, when you get to know me better, even though I have tried as best I can to show myself to you just as I am. But then I fell on my knees again and couldn't do anything but give thanks, thanks, and more thanks! O Emmy, how I thank you for your love! I don't believe you have any idea yet what it means to me. But eternity will show that, for through God's incomprehensible grace I believe we are indissolubly bound forever.

I thank you a thousand times, too, for your long, loving letter. Like yesterday's, it arrived early and brought me deep joy. I don't know why you feel you said too much – I think it was good that you expressed your views regarding social life, etc., so plainly. I agree with you point for point. "Put off the world, and put Christ on; that way the task is fully done," says an old rhyme.

As for prayer, whether a request is answered depends on two conditions:

1. Faith – that is, the certainty you have already beforehand that you will be answered. Faith comes through dedication to Christ. See, for instance, Matthew 21:21–22: "I tell you the truth, if you have faith and do not doubt, not only can you do what was done to the fig tree, but also you can say to this mountain, 'Go, throw yourself into the sea,' and it will be done. If you believe, you will receive whatever you ask for in prayer." Matthew 17:20: "...because you have so little faith. I tell you the truth, if you have faith as small as a mustard seed, you can say to this mountain, 'Move from here to there' and it will move. Nothing will be impossible for you." And James 1:5–8: "If any of you lacks wisdom, he should ask God, who gives generously to all without finding fault, and it will be given to him. But when he asks, he must believe and not doubt, because he who doubts is like a wave of the sea, blown and tossed by the wind. That man should not think he will receive anything from the Lord; he is a double-minded man, unstable in all he does."

   As a true Christian – and those are the only people we're talking about – I can have faith and certainty *only* when I am sure, through the Word and the Spirit, that my prayer is (in accordance with God's will) for wisdom (James 1:5), for grace (Romans 5:2), or for the Holy Spirit (Luke 11:13).

2. The second condition is referred to in the Bible by the phrase "in the name of Jesus"; that is, in his place, on his behalf, and with his purpose and Spirit, as if he himself were doing it. See, for example, John 14:12–13: "I tell you the truth, anyone who has faith in me will do what I have been doing. He will do even greater things than these, because I am going to the Father. And I will do whatever you ask in my name, so that the Son may bring glory to the Father." And John 16:23: "In that day you will no longer ask me anything. I tell you the truth, my Father will give you whatever you ask in my name."

This is of course possible only for someone who is fully converted, someone who is righteous; someone who has been renewed through Jesus and in whom Jesus lives and rules. See James 5:16: "Confess your sins to each other and pray for each other so that you may be healed. The prayer of a righteous man is powerful and effective."

You see then that such foolish prayers as asking that I should finish my last two years of study and receive my Ph.D. within a week, or that I should get 100,000 Marks, stand entirely outside the biblical way of thinking. Certainly, we can and ought to ask for earthly things, but always in the name and spirit of Jesus Christ, believing in him and his word and abandoning our self-will. If we want to understand and experience the scriptures, we must be utterly sincere in having surrendered ourselves totally to Jesus.

Matthew 7:7–11 is not talking about any and every request (after all, it advises us to seek and knock). Rather, as shown by the context, which must always be considered, it is talking about prayers firstly for the Holy Spirit's help in discernment and in caring for souls – Matthew 7:1–6. See also Luke 11:13: "If you then, though you are evil, know how to give good gifts to your children, how much more will your Father in heaven give the Holy Spirit to those who ask him."

Secondly, this chapter is about praying for entry into God's kingdom, and conversion to Jesus – Matthew 7:13–14: "Enter through the narrow gate. For wide is the gate and broad is the road that leads to destruction, and many enter through it. But small is the gate and narrow the road that leads to life, and only a few find it."

Now I've gotten completely carried away, though I only intended to write a little. I have a terrific amount of work to do before Saturday. Pray for me.

Just a few more things. Matthew 7:15–23 say clearly that it is not praying or doing great deeds that frees us from condemnation, but only submitting our will completely and absolutely to God, doing his will unwaveringly (verse 21), and believing in Jesus and his word (verse 24).

I would like to get the Siewerts' address from you, since I am to be staying with them. Betty will not be able to come with me, since she has to go to the dentist, among other things. She is looking forward to meeting you at Whitsun.

Loving you more and more in Jesus, and faithfully yours,

Ebbo

Baptism

Herr von Hollander's first encounter with his prospective son-in-law left him unimpressed. He disliked the young man's forward nature and, due to his own tenuous financial situation, worried for his daughter's future. Nevertheless, he gradually warmed up to Eberhard, and it wasn't long before Emmy could write, "Papa says he's taken you into his heart." Meanwhile she decided (at the urging of both her fiancé and Frau Baehr) to leave her nursing job and remain at home for the time being, in order to "deepen her conversion" – something she sought to do as well during Eberhard's next visit to Halle, when the young couple spent hours talking and reading and attending revival meetings.

Halle
April 27, 1907

My beloved Eberhard,

Thank you again for the many books – I plan to read all of them, little by little. I cannot read them quickly, though, so if you need one or the other of them back, I will send it. I have begun the one on Finney. It has made a tremendous impression on me so far, and I hope there'll be a blessing on it.

Yesterday evening we were at Herr Siewert's house with Fräulein von Nostiz, the Sallwürks, and a few others. The topic of infant baptism came up, and everyone said that according to the Bible it is not a valid practice. I am not at all certain. I must say that it doesn't seem very important to me. Up till now my view has been that Jesus instituted baptism in order to distinguish Christians from children of the world, and that whoever has been baptized has thus died with Christ. It's true that nowadays everyone's baptized as a child. But if we would allow ourselves to be re-baptized, we would remain the same in the view of the world – we would become "Christians," which is what we are already. I don't know if I've expressed myself clearly.

Else, on the other hand, feels fairly certain that infant baptism is not valid. She said yesterday that if she came to understand the matter more clearly, she would have herself re-baptized. At this Mama became furious (I had also said that if I recognized it as being in accordance to God's word, I would do it) and said it was blasphemy. She added that anyone who had herself baptized would be committing a grave sin and would not be allowed to remain in the house. She said she would not live under the same roof with someone who had been re-baptized and, reminding us of the commandment to honor father and mother, sternly forbade us even to entertain such an idea.

Today I am very sad about all this. Even though I clearly acknowledged that for the time being it was out of the question for me to be re-baptized, I insisted that I would unreservedly do the will of God as I recognized it, in his strength. Olga always tries to mediate. She finds Else and me too narrow-minded, though in many things she seems to understand us. Mama, by the way, also said she would forbid us from going to the meetings, as we are getting too wound up.

What do you think about baptism? In the Acts of the Apostles it says several times, "He had himself baptized with his whole household." At least now, I don't feel this is God's will for me. O Ebbo, pray about this, and also for Mama and Else (but don't write anything about it to Mama)! Now, one more question in regard to the Holy Spirit which worries me somewhat. I can't say that I've experienced a moment when I received the Holy Spirit, as for example Finney or Fräulein von Nostiz can, to the degree that (like them) I could not control myself for joy. I believe I know something of the Holy Spirit – how else could I now recognize so much that I did not see earlier in the Bible and in my life, and what else gives me the certainty of having a Savior?

But above all, I want to know how you are doing. How late do you work and on what? May God give you strength; without that, it can't be accomplished. Your studies are always in my prayers.

Oh, my Ebbo, I look forward so much to seeing you in Breslau. In three weeks we will really be together again, and then we can talk over so many things.

In faithful love,
your Emmy

Olga has just been to Pastor Hobbing's. She told him all about us, and he said he is in agreement with us in general, but not totally. He doesn't like Bernhard Kühn and his book, *Back to the First Love.* He said Kühn is an uneducated man. He finds it unconscionable that someone would talk to such young Christians about baptism and get them upset about it.

When the von Hollander parents realized that their daughters' questioning of accepted church teaching was more than just a phase, they were beside themselves. Frau von Hollander became so distraught that she said she'd kill herself if they were re-baptized. After all, such an act of apostasy would result in expulsion from the established church, and that meant far more than simply being struck from the membership rolls. In a society where the state church operated everything from schools and universities to hospitals and cemeteries, it would be social suicide. For young women of good breeding – women like the von Hollander sisters, whose family had loyally served state and church for generations – it would be an unthinkable scandal.

Breslau
April 28, 1907

My dearest Emmy,

There is so much that moves me today that I don't know how I'll ever end this letter. And I long for you so terribly! This morning at eight o'clock I went out on my bicycle, because I had no peace at home waiting for your letter. Then the mail carrier comes past the bridge. I jump off my bicycle and ask him for the mail, and he hands me – a magazine! Crestfallen, I ride on, out into the wonderful morning air. To right and left the new green grass is sprouting, and the sun shines, friendly and warm. I keep silently praying, "Lord, make me joyful in spite of it, even if I have no letter! And bless Emmy, and help me to thank you that she has so much to do for you that she cannot write!"

But it was terribly hard – I couldn't quite get over my disappointment, though it did improve because it was so glorious outdoors. I got off my bicycle by a little stream with beautiful woods and bushes and a lovely view across the fields, read Matthew 26, and prayed for you and myself. About ten o'clock I was back home again. Imagine how infinitely happy I was when I found two letters there with your beloved handwriting! Thank you for everything you wrote!

I also had to thank Jesus for the fact that you and Else have decided to do God's will in all circumstances, insofar as you understand his Word. True rebirth can never be without this kind of decisiveness. I am moved that the issue of baptism is confronting you so seriously. I pray urgently that God, and no one else, leads you. This issue is closely connected with the whole question of the outward form that the church of God should take, which we will talk about together sometime. Just now I took out my old notes on baptism, and looked through them, and wrote to Else – the letter is also intended for you.

I am so happy that, God willing, you will be with me in three weeks. How I long for that! This time, Emmy, please put together all the points and questions we need to talk over. Don't forget! If you follow my suggestion below, we will be reading John 3 together on Whitsunday. That is as follows: I would very much like to start on Mark the day after tomorrow, firstly for the sake of what I'm working on, and secondly for your sake. We'd be finished with it on May 16 and could then start John. I am now reviewing the Gospels – that is, comparing and studying the three synoptic Gospels (until May 16) – and then starting on John, all in Greek of course. In the mornings I read it only with my heart, and then later I work it through. I think it would be good for you also to read the Gospels thoroughly first (comparing them all with Luke), before starting with Acts and the Epistles. Please write to me right away if you are in agreement. The Gospel of Mark brings the acting and working of Jesus (less so his words) to our eyes in an uncommonly vivid way.

Thank you for asking in such detail about my studies. I have to say that I am dissatisfied with what I have accomplished this week. God gave me strength to establish something of a basis for my work in the coming weeks. But I still got far too little done. First I had to arrange a number of things here, take care of correspondence, etc. I basically have to set aside, at least for now, all the correspondence I brought along, a good deal of which has to do with my kingdom work in various places. In addition, I had things to prepare for the university; and thirdly, I didn't always have the energy I would have wished for. The last days were better, however. Joyfully forward! Let us believe and pray with greater earnestness, and I will achieve more and more every week. Oh, how I need your intercession!

As to the books, keep them for now. I have no time to read them. They are all significant. Finney was wholly decisive in making me determined to become a saver of souls for many – yes *many!* God used him on me. It is excellent that you are reading him now, and that he is making such an impression on you. Read his life first and his talks afterward. That's probably what you are planning anyway.

The fact that Finney – as well as our dear Fräulein von Nostiz and many others who belonged to God through the ages (above all, the apostles at Pentecost) – received the Holy Spirit in a way that involved powerfully stirred emotions and other outward signs must not make us think that the Spirit is limited to such accompanying phenomena. That is far from the case. No one can call Jesus "Lord" (and thus belong to him) except through the Holy Spirit, as it says in 1 Corinthians 12:3, Romans 8:9: "You, however, are controlled not by the sinful nature but by the Spirit, if the Spirit of God lives in you. And if anyone does not have the Spirit of Christ, he does not belong to Christ"; and 8:14: "because those who are led by the Spirit of God are sons of God." And *anyone* whom the Spirit of God guides and leads is God's child. For most, this comes about quite naturally and unnoticed, by means of the Word, sober reflection, and circumstances. Thus, for example, our engagement was undoubtedly a leading of the Holy Spirit. When we know Jesus, love Jesus, and follow Jesus, we have the Holy Spirit, for he shows and glorifies Jesus. See John 15:26: "When the Counselor comes, whom I will send to you from the Father, the Spirit of truth who goes out from the Father, he will testify about me"; and 16:13–14: "But when he, the Spirit of truth, comes, he will guide you into all truth. He will not speak on his own; he will speak only what he hears, and he will tell you what is yet to come. He will bring glory to me by taking from what is mine and making it known to you."

It is important, however, to distinguish here. The same Spirit who 1) makes his dwelling in every converted person and who glorifies Jesus wants 2) to take possession of that person and fill him so completely and utterly that he will be at his constant disposal as an instrument for others. This means being equipped with the Holy Spirit to serve. This was what gave Finney the strength to save so many thousands. And it is as a result that we are now seeing such a powerful awakening in Halle.

Finally, the Spirit wants 3) to use us to convince the world as to sin, justice, and judgment. See John 16:7–11: "I tell you the truth: It is for your good that I am going away. Unless I go away, the Counselor will not come to you; but if I go, I will send him to you. When he comes, he will convict the world of guilt in regard to sin and righteousness and judgment: in regard to sin, because men do not believe in me; in regard to righteousness, because I am going to the Father, where you can see me no longer; and in regard to judgment, because the prince of this world now stands condemned."

We are capable of service only through the Spirit. The more we have the Spirit, the more souls will we be able to rescue. And receiving the Spirit, who is a personage, will always be possible for us if we are surrendered to Jesus in faith. Yes, we do have him. Sometimes we are filled with the Spirit all of a sudden; but sometimes it happens gradually, as we allow ourselves to be detached more and more from self and grow to trust him only and totally. Let us pray, pray, pray for the Holy Spirit. It is actually very simple. It only appears to be a difficult question. I, too, was occupied by it for a long time before it became clear to me.

But now I must finally close as I have several other letters to write. When you wrote that Olga told Pastor Hobbing everything, surely you didn't mean that she said anything about our engagement? Please clarify this immediately! I'm praying especially for Olga. It seems to me that she lacks full trust, that she is afraid of things going badly if she obeys Jesus completely. That is not faith in the full sense – it is not faith at all. It is more like seeking and experimenting. Or am I being too skeptical?

Until Saturday evening, then. *Auf Wiedersehen!*
Loving and trusting you boundlessly,
your Eberhard

Halle
April 29, 1907

My Ebbo,

Today I received your long letter, and it gave me great joy and strength. If I have time today, I still want to write you a letter. But I would like to go to both meetings today.

Let's begin with Mark. I agree with your suggestion wholeheartedly!

Olga did not tell Pastor Hobbing anything about our engagement. She told him about Frau Baehr, Fräulein von Nostiz, and our discussion on baptism and the Lord's Supper. Papa says to greet you very warmly. I pray for you and your work constantly.

In Jesus,
your Emmy

Halle
April 30, 1907

My beloved Eberhard,

I got your sweet card today, which made me enormously happy. It was touching that you wrote to Olga too, and she wants to write back. Else also wants to write as soon as she's clear about the point of baptism. Yes, my Ebbo, I often long so very much for you, and I look forward terrifically to seeing you. I will put together a list of the things we must and shall talk over this time.

I am really confused about the question of the rapture. Essler spoke about it last night, and it seemed quite clear to me. All four of us were there. But then when we got home, Olga got all excited and told our parents how crazy it was that young people are having their heads turned by such far-fetched ideas, and she said she thought it was irresponsible to allow Monika to keep attending meetings with us. She told them that nothing at all was said about Jesus, and that Essler couldn't possibly know that Jesus would come soon. To her it was just religious madness. After this, my parents wanted to talk with me. I was quite calm about the whole thing, and they acknowledged this, and said that as I was sensible, the meetings wouldn't do me any harm. However, they said that my sisters will not be allowed to go anymore. (In the end, they did consent to Else and Monika going once a day.) But now I would like to know from *you* – can we really expect Jesus to come back soon?

Mama has forbidden virtually all contact with Fräulein von Nostiz. She complained that the first thing she heard about from "that lady" was the rapture, and – even more impossible – that our baptism as babies was not valid. Mama is so upset about this. Personally, I think it was stupid of Monika to tell her about all this right away. I'm still unsure of Olga's position.

By the way, my cousin has still not made a decision. She said she's always wanted to follow Jesus, so doesn't feel the need to be converted. I read some things to her about this, and she said she would think about them.

I hope your work isn't becoming too much for you. I continually pray that you'll be given strength for it. Yes, if we trust, God *will* give it. Are you any less pale?

Today I'm actually pretty busy, as the maid is still sick, so I can't write as much as I'd like. I have to get dinner ready now. More later.

Did I ever write about Fräulein Lodemann, Else's drawing instructor whom she liked so much? After her conversion, Else went and told her that she had given her life to Jesus and that now she is always happy. Her teacher laughed at her, and said she didn't believe it, and that she'd check back with her in half a year. But then a few days ago she came to Else and said, "I've been wanting to make you happy for a long time," and gave her the picture "Jesus and Nicodemus," by Sallwürk, and told her that the drawing had made a powerful impression on her. Now she also wants to come with us to the meetings. We really have to pray for her.

But now I must close. How are your dear mother and the others? Everyone here greets you warmly.

In deepest love,
your Emmy

Breslau
May 1, 1907

My endlessly beloved Emmy,

To begin with, warm thanks for your letters and for thinking of me so faithfully! Your letters move me deeply. Naturally I, too, think of you continually and pray especially for you, but also for all our loved ones, with great joy. I can jot down only a few points today, which are partially obvious:

1) Thanks to the Lord, my work is proceeding more and more successfully. Let's keep praying!
2) At times I feel strained but am generally joyful.
3) Mama is well, thanks to God. Everyone here sends warm greetings!

4) Be more obliging, more devoted, and more helpful than ever to your parents! Offer them your help around the house as much as you can and devote yourself to them.
5) Always be joyful, innocent, and natural! The Lord will grant everything.
6) Testify resolutely to Jesus' will, but avoid everything that is not demanded by him and does not serve him. My feeling is that Matthew 5:13–16 is more important for you than the rapture: "You are the salt of the earth. But if the salt loses its saltiness, how can it be made salty again? It is no longer good for anything, except to be thrown out and trampled by men. You are the light of the world. A city on a hill cannot be hidden. Neither do people light a lamp and put it under a bowl. Instead they put it on its stand, and it gives light to everyone in the house. In the same way, let your light shine before men, that they may see your good deeds and praise your Father in heaven."
7) Rather go only once a day, in the afternoon, to the meeting.
8) Olga ought to concentrate at home before Jesus.
9) Let nothing rob you of the quiet and peace of Jesus!

Your faithful Ebbo

Whenever something isn't clear to you, you can safely trust Jesus. He is peace.

Halle
May 10, 1907

My Ebbo,

Yesterday, Ascension Day, I unfortunately didn't manage to write. In the morning we heard a very good sermon by Pastor Wagner on Colossians 3:1–4. The essence of it was that if we want to be resurrected with Jesus – if he is to reveal his glory to us – then we must first die with him. He expounded on this in a very down-to-earth way. In the afternoon, Henny Zabeler spent time with us and tried to play the woman of the world. She wasn't very successful, however, and you could tell she was putting it on. In the evening Olga and I went to the Alliance meeting.

Oh, Ebbo, Else and I heard something really shocking in connection with Pastor Hobbing and Frau Baehr. We gathered from Mama that Pastor Hobbing told Olga about something that is simply impossible! I'd rather tell you about it directly, but I'm horrified. I can't figure Olga out. She is completely incomprehensible to me. She comes to all the meetings, but afterward she talks over everything that didn't please her with Mama, who really has no understanding for it at all.

Incidentally, Olga says she's repelled by our one-sidedness. I'm sure I've become one-sided, but I think that's natural, since I want to place myself solely on the side of Jesus.

I also want to tell you how often the devil tries to cause my downfall. For example, in the morning or at other times when I'm reading the Bible, he troubles me a great deal, causing me great anxiety. Often it's hours before I find peace again, though Jesus always conquers in the end.

Your letter made me very happy – especially that you have received more strength from the Lord for your work. But Ebbo, when you're overtired, you really shouldn't work so hard. God doesn't demand more than we're able to do.

What you wrote about your studies, by the way, makes things clearer to me. I've read quite a lot about early Christianity and the persecution of the first believers. Thinking of today in comparison to that era, there are several questions I want to ask you. I also want to talk with you about the church.

Yesterday Else asked our parents for permission to be baptized. She told me she'll wait a month, but then intends to go ahead anyway. As you can imagine, our parents are furious and have strictly forbidden Else to go to any meetings, to Frau Baehr, or to Fräulein von Nostiz.

In deep love,
your faithful Emmy

As time went on, it became clearer and clearer that Pastor Hobbing, although a longtime von Hollander acquaintance, was no friend of the awakening sweeping through Halle. Alleging fanaticism on the part of its leaders, he also spread gossip questioning their moral integrity, particularly that of Frau Baehr.

Breslau
May 11, 1907

My Emmy,

I'm very thankful for your darling letters, because they let me experience everything with you and allow me to pray with you in everything you encounter.

I'm writing you today for two reasons, but first and foremost because of what you indicated regarding Pastor Hobbing and Frau Baehr. It strengthens my opinion of Hobbing, which is now much worse than it was earlier. (Don't give Olga any inkling of this!)

Dear Emmy, what we're concerned with here is a friend and sister in Jesus, and the honor of our Lord, but also the relationship of trust among his disciples. So the matter – whatever it may be – cannot be postponed, but *must* be cleared up, absolutely and immediately. 1 Corinthians 13:6: "Love does not delight in evil but rejoices with the truth" applies here, and even more, Matthew 18:15–17: "If your brother sins against you, go and show him his fault, just between the two of you. If he listens to you, you have won your brother over. But if he will not listen, take one or two others along, so that 'every matter may be established by the testimony of two or three witnesses.' If he refuses to listen to them, tell it to the church; and if he refuses to listen even to the church, treat him as you would a pagan or a tax collector."

Someone has sinned. Consequently it is first Olga's, then Else's, your, and Monika's, and finally my duty to clear up the matter with relentless straightforwardness. Olga must talk the matter over clearly with Frau Baehr, or else she is not submitting to the word of Jesus, and is therefore subject to Matthew 7:24–27 where it speaks of the wise and foolish builders, also especially verse 21: "Not everyone who says to me, 'Lord, Lord,' will enter the kingdom of heaven, but only he who does the will of my Father who is in heaven." If Olga doesn't do this – if she doesn't clear her accusation against a Christian woman – then you and your other sisters are obliged to demand a clear word from her. If you do not find the way forward, I myself shall energetically take the matter in hand, and this would be unpleasant.

My beloved little Emmy, I think my point is clear. By means of this way, in obedience to Matthew 18, I have often accomplished tremendous things to the praise of Jesus and to the disgrace of the enemy. No compromise is possible.

By the way, it's an old story that disciples living in the strength of the Spirit are constantly slandered, as for example in Matthew 5:11: "Blessed are you when people insult you, persecute you and falsely say all kinds of evil against you because of me." Disgusting lies have been disseminated about von Gerdtell, and also about von Viebahn, Modersohn, Girkon, et al. About me – keep this to yourself – people have claimed that I stole money from my parents' safe, and other absurdities as well. And my uncle, Pastor Klein, once had eighteen or nineteen lawsuits and disciplinary measures taken against him in one year because of his witness against sin. In some of these cases, the lies were even supported by perjury. But Jesus vindicated him.

So remain as calm as you are resolute and thorough. And *pray!*

The second reason I'm writing you today is that tomorrow after seven o'clock I'm giving a talk to up to one hundred young people – fourteen to eighteen years old – in which I am supposed to show them the way to the Savior. Please pray specifically that at least some may be visibly rescued and reborn. We have been promised this!

I'm very glad, Emmy, if you're becoming one-sided, in the sense you wrote. Let us live only for Jesus; read, speak, and act only for him and for no one else, and not even for the noblest ideal. Oh, how rich life becomes through Jesus' poverty! Look at 2 Corinthians 8:9: "For you know the grace of our Lord Jesus Christ, that though he was rich, yet for your sakes he became poor, so that you through his poverty might become rich"; John 15:16: "You did not choose me, but I chose you and appointed you to go and bear fruit – fruit that will last. Then the Father will give you whatever you ask in my name"; and 10:11: "I am the good shepherd. The good shepherd lays down his life for the sheep."

Emmy, let us be joyful, unaffected, innocent, natural, and unforced in our determination. This is very important; otherwise we'll fall under pressure of the law and not the Holy Spirit. The spirit of Jesus is a spirit of freedom; that is, of voluntary, joyful obedience in the strength of faith. (See Romans and Galatians.) So never allow yourself to be controlled by moods and depressions sent by the enemy. Instead, look to Jesus and go your way quietly, ignoring Satan, as you have done away with him. Hebrews 12:2: "Let us fix our eyes on

Jesus, the author and perfecter of our faith, who for the joy set before him endured the cross, scorning its shame, and sat down at the right hand of the throne of God."

I'm so sad about Olga. I was about to write you nearly two weeks ago that I think she's in a crisis, and that if she doesn't make up her mind to serve Jesus alone, she could become our worst enemy. I write this with pain. Let's pray, *pray* that it turns out differently.

I'm glad Monika is taking things seriously. It's essential that she does, or she won't be able to withstand the struggles of the coming months. It's going to get serious.

Despite all this, over and over again, remember 2 Corinthians 2:14, in regard to everybody and everything: "But thanks be to God, who always leads us in triumphal procession in Christ and through us spreads everywhere the fragrance of the knowledge of him."

By the way, I take baptism very seriously; I've never considered it a secondary matter. It's only that my understanding of it was different until now. In my leaflets I tried to present the nature and significance of nominal Christianity and its limitation through infant baptism. See Romans 3:9 concerning individual sects (their salvation): "What shall we conclude then? Are we any better? Not at all! We have already made the charge that Jews and Gentiles alike are all under sin." And see 3:1–3 concerning the generality (the *possibility* of their salvation): "What advantage, then, is there in being a Jew, or what value is there in circumcision? Much in every way! First of all, they have been entrusted with the very words of God. What if some did not have faith? Will their lack of faith nullify God's faithfulness?" According to these verses, baptism is not invalid, but willed by Jesus and God. If the individual wishes to possess the saving power that is offered to all, he *must* experience circumcision of the heart (conversion) and baptism by the Holy Spirit.

That's been my stand until now. But let's review it together, my dear bride. We are, of course, both prepared to obey Jesus, whatever his word.

What a lot we have to talk about! It's high time you came. What happened with Frau Köhler?

Christ was active already before his incarnation – see 1 Corinthians 10:1–4: "For I do not want you to be ignorant of the fact, brothers, that our forefathers were all under the cloud and that they all passed through the sea. They were all baptized into Moses in the cloud and in the sea. They all ate the same spiritual food and drank the same spiritual drink; for they drank from the spiritual rock that accompanied them, and that rock was Christ"; John 1:4: "In him was life, and that life was the light of men"; and 9: "The true light that gives light to every man was coming into the world." A number of Old Testament believers like Enoch definitely lived in fellowship with God through the proleptic power of the death of Christ, otherwise they would have had no forgiveness. Jesus Christ, yesterday and today and the same into eternity! And (1 Corinthians 13:12) everything face to face! May the Lord let us grow in grace and understanding.

We still need to write each other with exact travel arrangements. I'm enclosing two letters and some poems for you to pass on. If you have time, copy them out for Frau Baehr and Else and keep the originals for yourself.

Looking forward to seeing you with inexpressibly great love, as to no other human being ever, into eternity.

Your Eberhard

Tomorrow I will catch up on my work. Greet everyone, especially your parents. Everybody sends their greetings.

Halle
May 12, 1907

My Ebbo,

I just received your dear letter. You can imagine that the matter with Pastor Hobbing and Frau Baehr stirred me up a great deal and continues to do so. I'll write in detail – you'll see that it's very difficult to do anything.

Olga was with Pastor Hobbing and talked everything over with him. Afterward she told us what had transpired, except for one thing, which she said she would *not* tell us. Last Thursday when Else said she had decided to be baptized, there was, of course, a terrible upheaval. Mama attacked Fräulein von Nostiz, who had introduced this "terrible subject," and also laid into Frau Baehr. Mama said it was unbelievable that she made "propaganda" about baptism; that she was extremely vain; and that she acted very differently toward men than toward ladies. I was naturally shocked and felt she was alluding to Pastor Hobbing.

Else told me later that Frau Baehr once asked her whether Pastor Hobbing ever flattered Olga. He does, which confirms something Olga said to me some time ago (she'd deny it now), that it sometimes seemed to her as if Pastor Hobbing was courting her, but that he always fought the temptation because he realized it was a sin.

Yesterday Mama went to Pastor Hobbing's to ask him for advice about the question of baptism, and while she was gone I spoke with Olga, who declared her great trust in Pastor Hobbing. This made me so indignant that I stated I myself had no trust whatsoever in him, because I believed I knew something horrible about him, through Mama. Olga said she didn't know what Mama was talking about. She said Pastor Hobbing had told her nothing, and she considered Frau Baehr a serious Christian woman. When Mama returned, we spoke with her, and she now says that perhaps she only imagined it or heard it from somebody else. So nothing can really be done.

Else had resolved to speak with Frau Baehr about Pastor Hobbing, but now she, too, says that nothing can be done about the matter. Of course I'm ready to do *anything*. What do *you* think? What I have written is only for you, by the way, but it makes me terribly sad, since there must be *something* behind all of this, and it seems that we're not hearing the real story.

I'm worried that Olga is going to be greatly harmed by all this since she hasn't yet placed herself undividedly on Jesus' side, in my opinion. Whenever she feels disquieted, she allows Mama to calm her down with trivial things.

Please think how to settle this matter with God's help. We're being talked out of *everything* we bring up in our desire to resolve this conflict and are being made into liars. We're being told that we've imagined everything. Nevertheless Else or I still plan to ask Frau Baehr herself what went on between her and Pastor Hobbing. O Ebbo, let's keep praying, especially for Olga. You know, she's terribly touchy, because she's noticed that we don't really trust her. Write to her sometime; she'll be won over only by love.

By the way, she's always saying, "You don't consider me converted, I suppose..." Don't be surprised that I keep coming back to this matter; it's going through my head practically all day long.

Another thing: my parents are suggesting that it might not suit your family to have me come at Whitsun. You know how Papa is!

This morning Olga, Monika, and I were at the Sallwürks for bible study. Director Siewert was there too. Else isn't allowed to go anymore, as you know. We wrote a letter to Herr von Viebahn, asking him to come to Halle in May or June to hold a lecture series here similar to von Gerdtell's. We all signed it, and many others are still going to sign it too.

I'm looking forward so eagerly to seeing you and to talking over *everything* with you, especially baptism. I have a great deal more to tell you.

Don't be surprised if Papa writes, asking you to try as hard as you can to dissuade us, especially Else, from baptism. He is trying *everything* to prevent it. He says he'd sooner have her placed under psychiatric care. We are staying completely calm, however. If it's God's will, he will guide it – he can always open doors. We said this to Papa, and he replied, "You talk the greatest nonsense and then say that God will guide it!" If Papa writes to you, pray that you do what is right in God's eyes.

Everyone greets you, especially Else, who thanks for your letter. She says to tell you she's very happy.

Loving you more than anyone in the world, after Jesus,
your faithful Emmy

Breslau
May 13, 1907

My beloved Emmy,

Warm thanks for your loving, detailed letter. I'm sorry for all you've had to go through, and I empathize with you. But it's good, Emmy, that we are in the midst of the fire, because struggle is a sign of life. Let us persevere in joyful faith! We won't turn aside one millimeter from the clearly recognized way of Jesus. And should we be forced, through obedience to him, to bring on further conflicts, we can do nothing else but continue on his way, without a single concession to the right or left. It's tremendous that we are at one in this – and I know, and knew, that you are ready for anything.

As things stand, the way is already difficult. I still maintain, however, that something more has to happen. I have prayed over it and reflected on it a great deal. I think your mother must either take back her statements or let us know what caused her to make them. I'm afraid you'll have a hard time accomplishing either clarification. Or what do you think? I also believe that it's only right that I give a firm witness on behalf of Frau Baehr.

I won't write anything about Olga, though I'd be glad of an opportunity to write *to* her again. I'm praying very earnestly for her.

I won't say anything about Pastor Hobbing today either. I've already prayed a great deal for him, alone and with others in Halle, and am praying for him now. I'm very sorry for him.

My mother's been meaning to write you for some time now, but she's been very busy. Today she hosted a big tea party. I fled to my room as soon as I could and then went to an event at the YMCA. Many of the young men there – I don't know the exact number – confessed their sins both personally and in a meeting afterward and committed their lives to Jesus. At the end they got up, one after another, and praised and glorified the Savior. Shouldn't we go down on our knees to give thanks that, on the prayer of his weak children, God performs such miracles again and again? Our whole life ought to be a song of praise. Hallelujah!

Emmy, may the Lord be close to you with his peace, which passes understanding. Thank your brother and your sisters for their greetings. I thank God again and again, from the depths of my heart, that you love me so much, and for our inexpressibly amazing relationship. Every word you write makes me rejoice. I'm actually unworthy to enjoy such great happiness!

But that's how it is with everything that Jesus gives, and that's why we love him above all else.

Loving you above all others in the world,
your Eberhard

Halle
May 13, 1907

My Ebbo,

Yes, finally I can understand why it says in the Bible, "I did not come to bring peace, but a sword." We've been having scenes here almost all day long now. This morning Mama spoke very firmly with me and asked me to help her prevent Else from being baptized. I'm supposed to get you to do the same. I told her I can't do this, since I'd never prevent Else from fulfilling God's will as she recognizes it, and since I'm wondering whether I, too, should have myself baptized.

I'm convinced God will guide it all wonderfully. But my parents won't stop at anything, even if it means setting the whole world in motion to dissuade her. They want 1) to write to Herr von Viebahn, 2) to warn the preacher against baptizing Else, 3) to write to Herr Baehr and call him to account because his wife "dishonored and deceived us" by not informing our parents that she was a re-baptizer. Mama claims Frau Baehr came to us under false pretenses. She claims Frau Baehr creeps into houses to entice children away from their parents, which she and Papa call Jesuitism. They also want 4) to write to you, and 5) to make the matter public. They are even considering publishing a warning in the newspapers against Frau Baehr and Fräulein von Nostiz. Well, that last one might actually serve the honor of Jesus: "Though all should fall and break, God never shall forsake." Papa, by the way, says he's going to search the Bible so that he can form his own judgment.

Just now there was a bad incident with Else: Mama attacked certain serious believers we know, and Else defended them fiercely. I stayed calm – I just said Mama's accusations weren't true. But Mama got very angry at Else and told her she'd completely forgotten the commandment to honor father and mother. For her part, Else doesn't know whether she's right in defending everything so passionately. I myself think she should be calmer, since our parents know her point of view anyway. I thank God when he gives me peace. How can I be angry with my parents anyway? After all, they don't understand us in the least, and in their own eyes they are only acting out of love for us.

Your letters and poems strengthen me very much. O Ebbo, pray, pray for strength for me and Else and Monika. Olga is *not* acting rightly, but we should also pray that she comes to Jesus. She told Monika yesterday that while she doesn't want to do anything against Jesus, she's still going to go ahead and do what isn't expressly against him. She's not only sticking completely to our parents on the question of baptism, but is encouraging them on as well. We *must* pray her out of this.

Loving you endlessly, and praying for you,
your faithful Emmy

Breslau
May 15, 1907

My beloved Emmy,

I wouldn't have thought the fight would become almost as hot with your family as with mine. It's wonderful that before all these events God led us twice in conversation to talk about the persecution of his followers! It's marvelous, actually: even the very noblest person can't stay neutral and friendly – in fact, he's the very one who can't. One must decide *for* or *against* Christ! *With* those who belong to him or *against* them! Anything else is a wretched whitewashing of death and decay. And anyone who makes the pitiful attempt to go along with both sides plays the saddest part; he'll find himself in nothing but impossible situations. Yes, let's pray that God opens every eye. I am doing this.

Here in Breslau, dear Emmy, you'll find things quiet, outwardly. But the powder keg could blow up again at the next spark. After bitter struggles, the most extensive liberties have been granted to me through God-given victory. I trust he'll give more and more each time. There are, of course, great differences from victory to victory. The unconverted members of my family have become increasingly unhappy in the years since my conversion, and it often tears at my heart. Outwardly, they are quite prosperous (Papa's estimated income is 9,000 Marks, and his property is worth about 70,000 – 80,000). And outwardly, to the world, they seem reasonably happy. But inwardly there is terrible strife and unpeace. Those of us in our family who seriously believe in Christ need to take a more decisive stand. Then, only then, will the others make a decision. At least that's how it seems to me. I'll tell you all about it in greater detail. How will we ever get through all that we have to say to each other? I don't believe we ever will.

My dear little Emmy, it is surely already clear to you that you have a great task from the Lord ahead of you with regard to my family, especially Clara and Hannah. Both are looking forward to your fellowship very much. I'm confident that your joyful, loving nature and your unaffected, resolute witness will win hearts for Jesus. But we must also pray for this, humbly and earnestly, since we know that he alone can grant it. He *wants* it.

You're arriving at 9:41 Saturday evening, at the main station, right? Let me know what class you're traveling, and which hat and jacket you'll be wearing, and sit by the window if possible. You'll get out on the left. I'll be there with either Hannah or Clara, and after we let the train pass, we'll walk toward the first car until we find you. Remain in the train, or stand in front of your car – that way we can't miss each other, even in a crowd. I'll be wearing a dark overcoat, white neck scarf, and derby. I'll wave my hat. All clear?

I have a lot to tell you about church history. Above all, many thanks for your photo, the poems, and the letter. You've made me so happy!

In great love,
your Ebbo

Joy in the Lord

In pre-war Germany, Whitsun (Pentecost) marked the beginning of summer, not only for churchgoers, but also for university students, who looked forward to their first holiday in hiking weather. In 1907, Emmy spent these days in Breslau with Eberhard and his family. Although the Arnolds received her warmly, they privately tried to get her to nudge their son away from his (to them) worrisome religious zeal and onto the path toward middle-class security. In one whispered conversation, Frau Arnold divulged the extremes to which her "misguided" son had gone in the past: "He even wanted to join the Salvation Army!" she told Emmy. "You never know what he might do next in his enthusiasm and his love of Christ and the poor." Meanwhile, Eberhard himself was primarily chained to his books, preparing for his doctoral examinations in theology and working on his thesis.

Halle
June 7, 1907

My dearest, beloved Ebbo,

I didn't manage to write you yesterday, because I spent several hours with Frau Baehr. She didn't mention our letter once, but questioned me about you, etc. I wasn't able to tell her much, as we were interrupted by Fräulein Weddy-Pönicke. She told me, by the way, that she is finished with Christianity. I asked her whether she was happy, to which she replied, "At the moment." I told her that that wouldn't be sufficient for me; that Jesus says, "He who drinks of this water will not thirst again," and "Whoever believes in me has eternal life. He will not be judged, nor will he see death forever." Not that this made any visible impression on her – she began arguing, and as you know, I'm not qualified for that. So I went away and visited Fräulein Köhler, who has been ill since her return from Breslau. I got the impression that she now regrets her conversion – she seemed to be afraid of any serious discussion. I told her I'd come again on Saturday or Sunday, and she replied that I shouldn't be angry with her if she put me off, but often a visit just didn't suit her. I replied that I wouldn't take it badly, but that it would make me happy if I could visit her.

I could be mistaken, but I am rather anxious about her; and I also reproach myself somewhat, quite a lot in fact, for not having concerned myself enough with her and for praying too little for her. On Sunday I'll go again, and pray earnestly beforehand. I'd actually prefer to remain quiet, so that I myself can get further, and so that God can disclose to me the many things that I must still get rid of so as to be able to give myself completely into death. There must still be something – or many things – in me that hinder the spirit of God. But as God wills! It's only that I feel myself so terribly unworthy.

I often reproach myself – when, for example, I've talked about the experiences of others (e.g. yours) and treated them as fact simply because I believed them, even though I myself haven't yet experienced them personally.

Yesterday somebody in the Alliance class said that one doesn't need to experience everything, but that we are allowed to take everything in faith – and then the personal experience will come. What do you think, my Ebbo? I've wondered about this a great deal, and it has brought me to prayer. Pray for me that I will find clarity. It's definitely the devil that makes me afraid. I always think of 1 Peter 5:8–9: "Your enemy the devil prowls around like a roaring lion looking for someone to devour. Resist him, standing firm in the faith, because you know that your brothers throughout the world are undergoing the same kind of sufferings." And 1 Peter 2:25: "For you were like sheep going astray, but now you have returned to the Shepherd and Overseer of your souls." These and other words give me renewed strength, as does Isaiah 43:1: "But now, this is what the Lord says – he who created you, O Jacob, he who formed you, O Israel: 'Fear not, for I have redeemed you; I have summoned you by name; you are mine.'" And 43:4: "Since you are precious and honored in my sight, and because I love you, I will give men in exchange for you, and people in exchange for your life." I find Ezekiel 3:17–19 very serious, by the way: "Son of man, I have made you a watchman for the house of Israel; so hear the word I speak and give them warning from me. When I say to a wicked man, 'You will surely die,' and you do not warn him or speak out to dissuade him from his evil ways in order to save his life, that wicked man will die for his sin, and I will hold you accountable for his blood. But if you do warn the wicked man and he does not turn from his wickedness or from his evil ways, he will die for his sin; but you will have saved yourself."

I keep repeating to myself: "I can do nothing at all, but Jesus can do everything. The less I am, the more Jesus can do in me."

Now I'd like to know how your studies are going and how *you* are. I'm so glad we're reading Luke together. I was especially happy to see the word "convert" twice in today's reading, since I want to prove to Olga that the expression is biblical. I'm copying out many passages and already have quite a number. I'm also eager to read the Letter to the Romans. If I could copy out your poems, or any other things you want to have printed, now while I have time, I'd be very happy to, so you can work.

I also want to write to Clara soon. I love her very much. How are your dear parents? Olga was very happy with your card and plans to answer you soon. Else is still in bed. She's calm, though, and has decided not to have herself secretly baptized after all, until a year is up.

I can't get close to Heinz at all. He wants to become a Catholic, though I think he just wants to make himself interesting. Recently he said he hadn't taken communion there yet, nor would he do so. He thinks that because Else wants to be baptized (and will therefore become a Baptist in his eyes), he has the right to become a Catholic. At the same time he tells such stupid jokes. For example, he compares the story of Jonah and the whale with Little Red Riding Hood and the wolf, and says he doesn't believe either of them. He's superficial about everything and totally mixed up. The only thing that will rescue him is conversion, so we have to pray for him.

Monika is sticking with us, though tomorrow she's going to the Rose Festival, a big charity ball that is being promoted all over. I hope it doesn't do her any harm. You pray about it too. I suppose God can use it to bind her more firmly to himself if she realizes that it's just empty frivolity.

This is getting to be a very long letter. Tomorrow I'll be at Lucia Franke's. I'll be good to her – after all, we're sisters in Jesus – and will probably suggest that we read something together. Think of me.

Praying for you in deepest love,
your Emmy

Breslau
June 9, 1907

Jesus!

Emmy, my darling,

It's been terribly hard not to write for so long. Every fiber urged me to, and I had so much to tell you. But it was the Lord's will (and also what you wanted), so I think it was a victory. As a result I managed, through his strength, to work completely through the Gospel of John and Schlatter's book on it this week. I finished at about 11:30 last night. That caught me up on the study time missed because of our wonderful time together. It would be excellent if I was able to work through the New Testament by the beginning of August, since during the holidays and the winter semester I must concentrate solely on church history, the Old Testament, and other subjects that are almost as urgent. Next week I'll work through the Letters of Paul again. I have to get through one or two books on the Letter to the Romans.

When did *you* start on Romans? Please let me know immediately. Begin on Monday if you haven't yet. If it's too much, time-wise, or for any other reason, just limit yourself to Luke. I also intend to take up the Psalms again this week. I'll need a lot of strength to see it all through. But it always helps me enormously that you pray for me as you do.

This week I critiqued a very poor sermon and received a fine commendation from Professor Karre. After the sermon and my extremely negative criticism of it, the student who'd given it asked if he could walk home with me. He opened up more and more as we talked, and in the end he unburdened his whole heart to me. He said he'd experienced nothing of what he was preaching about, though he knew it was the truth. He felt quite clearly that he needed to be converted, but he couldn't let this happen before the end of the semester, since he had another important obligation to fulfill, which would conflict with it (something to do with being officer of a student club or maybe even a duel!). But he now said he would decide immediately and completely for Christ as soon as he'd fulfilled the other obligation. He's the head officer in a thirty-man fraternity, a good drinker, and an excellent swordsman. But he repeatedly told me that all this (and really the whole world) is actually hollow and repugnant to him.

You can imagine how I thanked God for this wonderful opportunity and for giving me strength to tell this man the truth sharply and with love. The unhappy man! Postponement could easily be his ruin.

Now, however, my fine, beloved bride, I'm going to tell you all the things I have on my heart, one after the other. You know that I want my whole heart to be yours so completely that you know everything in it, and will finally know more about it than even I. Maybe this is already the case.

I am concerned, though, that you greatly overestimate me, and I don't want that. You must be my helper in such a way that I gain full mastery over myself, also in those areas where I don't yet see clearly. I'm sure there are plenty of those! I know that you'll want to do this. I'm indescribably thankful for the way you point me upward, and I will praise Jesus for it my whole life long and into eternity. I have an inexpressibly deep longing to take you into myself absolutely, with all that you think and feel, so that through your soul, my wonderful bride, I may be drawn ever higher toward the Lord.

Your letters are so valuable to me that, next to my Bible, they are my greatest treasure. It occurred to me today that through the very fact of being separated, we will be greatly blessed: we will always have our letters from this glorious time.

But now I must come down to earth and tell you everything else I'm thinking about. I'll begin with what is most important to me – you.

I'm so happy, my love, that you could write, "The less I am, the more Jesus can do in me," and that you repeatedly express your complete trust in him.

I have laid before the Lord what you wrote about your fear that there's something in you that hinders the Spirit. But I think you should let go of such gloomy brooding. If you're downcast and feel burdened by your sins and your incapacity to serve – if the sort of mood overcomes you in which the Enemy seems to sow doubt in your heart about whether you're saved – then, Emmy, go to Jesus as you are, as a poor, weak human child, and praise, honor, and thank him for granting full salvation even to the most wretched soul. *You* don't need to do anything. God gives us everything. Ask his forgiveness for having grieved him by mistrust (as if he demanded more than openness) and thank him that forgiveness is yours, since you've been redeemed by his death. Then ask him to relentlessly show you everything that is evil about yourself, and tell him firmly that you want to give it all up immediately. Finally, reflect quietly and do what you have to do in joyful confidence in him, fully determined to do whatever it takes, and assured of forgiveness and grace even before you've carried anything out. If the Lord doesn't show you anything, that's all the more reason to be truly joyful! By this he's telling you, "Rejoice in my grace! I know you love me, and I am in you. In my time, the right time, I will show you everything and lead you onward." Then continue on your way full of joy and thanks.

Little darling: be joyful! And realize that if you're not, you're disgracing Jesus. Doesn't each of us always have reason to rejoice? Yes, always rejoice! If the longing for me tries to rob you of your happiness, then bring it before Jesus and thank him that I am completely yours and that our souls are one, even at a distance. One more thing: the answers to some of your questions were already clear to you from the pamphlet, "Advice for the Newly Awakened." So don't let yourself be robbed of what the Lord has given, but use it instead to bear even more glorious fruit.

Trust in the Lord also in regard to the Holy Spirit. Believe that he *has* given it to you, and will, as often as you need it. If what God has in mind for you is silence, the Spirit will give you insights into yourself and Jesus, and won't give you strength to evangelize and save many people. If he wants to lead you to one soul, he'll give you just enough strength to enable you to witness to him in weakness. It isn't we who determine our service, but the Spirit, and this happens in the most natural way. Else can be filled with the Holy Spirit just as much while lying in bed as can the evangelist through whom hundreds might be finding their way to Jesus at the same time. In God's eyes the smallest, quietest service or act of obedience is worth just as much as the mightiest deed of faith. In fact, the latter isn't always as important as the former.

Let us become quiet, my dearest, and go our way in joy, praying earnestly for God's spirit, trusting him in every service we undertake, and thus glorifying Jesus by our peace. *That* is my prayer for you, my best beloved, and I know that the Lord will answer it and make you a witness who will praise and glorify him with her whole life!

By now you'll be able to see that it's none other than the devil who gives you unrest. See John 15:11: "I have told you this so that my joy may be in you and that your joy may be complete"; 14:26–27: "But the Counselor, the Holy Spirit, whom the Father will send in my name, will teach you all things and will remind you of everything I have said to you. Peace I leave with you; my peace I give you. I do not give to you as the world gives. Do not let your hearts be troubled and do not be afraid"; and 8:36: "So if the Son sets you free, you will be free indeed." You'll also see clearly that you certainly have a right to witness to the truth even if you haven't experienced the greatest things. Our guide is the Word, not our experiences. John 17:17: "Sanctify them by the truth; your word is truth." Please explain what you meant by this. Surely you'll always have enough of Jesus to be able to witness to that!

My Emmy, I hope you've finally stopped relying on feelings. Faith stands on the Word and thereby on the cross and the resurrection. The rock is outside of us, not in us. Psalm 40:2–4: "He lifted me out of the slimy pit, out of the mud and mire; he set my feet on a rock and gave me a firm place to stand. He put a new song in my mouth, a hymn of praise to our God. Many will see and fear and put their trust in the Lord. Blessed is the man who makes the Lord his trust, who does not look to the proud, to those who turn aside to false gods." (Of course, the Lord is also in us.)

I've been worried about Fräulein Köhler for some time already. Like you, I believe you haven't been loyal enough. Learn from this that the newly converted must be nurtured with the same care as newborn babies. They must never be left untended, even for a week. All kinds of temptations and thoughts will storm in upon them while they are still very tender. Perhaps the bud hasn't even really burst open in them yet, much as it seems to us that it has. And steadfastness is needed then as well. Let's hope – I'll pray for it – that the matter with Fräulein Köhler can still be put to rights.

Promise me that you'll take care of yourself and not neglect yourself in any way. And by the way, please do something about your eye inflammation. It seems to me that you often neglect your own needs. Please don't, for my sake.

I'm very glad that you have contact with Lucia Franke. God bless you, and her. Just be very tactful and cautious. I'll write a card to Herr Franke sometime and clarify my position. How did it go on Sunday?

I'd be very glad for your help with copying – my heartiest thanks for your offer. You'll soon see the article in the *Alliance News*.

Give Monika my thanks for her loving letter. I don't really mind that my letter to her was opened before she saw it, but I don't think it was proper. Still, your parents have the right to do what they want.

Do you think that perhaps Monika adapts herself too much to circumstances? She ought to go to Pastor Vonhof more often (I won't say anything about Pastor Hobbing) and try to fellowship, at least now and then, with other serious Christians. These dances really worry me. Does she herself dance? Does she confess to Jesus at such events? Does she go in his service, on a task for him? See Colossians 3:17: "And whatever you do, whether in word or deed, do it all in the name of the Lord Jesus, giving thanks to God the Father through him"; and 2 Corinthians 5:15: "And he died for all, that those who live should no longer live for themselves but for him who died for them and was raised again." A "charity" ball – what hypocrisy! You must definitely let Monika act independently, in accordance with her own conscience, but you should still talk it over with her sometime.

I'll be writing to Else still today, if possible. Make sure that the others don't see the letter. It's for *her.* Poor Heinz! I'm going to write to him too. By the way, please write to Hannah. She's in Hamburg, in a very nice, orthodox Christian home, which could have a somnolent effect. Clara wrote me that she's having difficulties and needs wisdom and courage. Let us pray for her. (She'll be glad to send you more photographs – just write and ask her.)

Betty was recently asked, at a party, if my strict Christianity was causing a rift between her and her siblings. (People don't consider her one of us.) She replied, "Not in the least! You don't have to talk about things like that!" I thought her sweet answer unchristian, even though friendly, and told her that I'd actually love to talk with her about Jesus, the sooner the better. She laughed at this, friendly and tactful as ever, though clearly not liking what I had said.

Not long ago I made it clear to Papa, Mama, and Betty that I only consider people who live completely for Jesus to be Christians, and that I think there are very few Christians left in the established church. Betty took the opposite position: she thinks that if a person always goes to church and does his duty during the week, even if he doesn't think about Jesus too often, he will die "saved." I also told Mama and Betty that the reason I'd like to join the Salvation Army is that then I wouldn't be praised. Betty didn't understand this at all, and Mama said it was a subservient attitude. She said that good people should be recognized, or something like that.

I'd like to have a more thorough talk with Betty. Keep praying for her! Today I told her I wished she would use her singing entirely for the Lord. She cheerfully laughed off the idea: "You think I should drop singing other songs? You have no idea what a pleasure they are." I told her life is much richer when it is lived totally for Jesus – that no greater wealth can be found. She said she didn't believe this and certainly couldn't imagine herself singing in revival meetings. She told me my ideas were "Salvation Army ideas" and that I was unmusical, which is why I wouldn't understand. Besides, she claimed that she *does* sing for the Lord. Well, I'll go on having faith for her. Jesus conquers!

I have to close. I am well – the glorious kingly power of Jesus is my support. It's too splendid to live in his fellowship!

Recently we had a wonderful bible class about waiting for him. I trust in him fully, for my future as well. He will lead us surely and clearly and prepare a sun-bright way for us. I pray for you with joy, and love you more and more, if that's possible.

Belonging unreservedly to you,
your bridegroom

P. S. I am fine. I just scraped my knee falling off my bicycle. Greet everyone a thousand times. This letter will surely do for a week. You'll get a shorter one in the meantime anyway, though.

Halle
June 10, 1907

My most beloved Ebbo,

Your long, loving letter moved me, as did the poem. You love me so much! Know that I love you too – so much that I can't express it in words.

I'm glad you were able to do so much work in the last week. Thanks to the Lord for this. May he always give you more energy to serve him. I began reading Romans on Friday. It's rather hard for me to understand, especially the first half of chapter 3, though I know we once discussed this passage in connection with the question of baptism.

The witness you gave to that student is really splendid; it's wonderful how God leads. If only the young man would decide completely for Jesus!

Monika, Olga, and I just returned from the churchyard, where we heard an awful burial address by Pastor Fischer of St. John's parish. He stirringly described the deceased man's loyalty to his profession and his ideal family life (his greatest happiness) and said, among other things, that there is "room in the smallest hovel for a happy and loving couple." He praised the man as much as anyone can praise another person. At the end, he said the man had most likely prepared himself for death and was now in the faithful arms of the Savior, since Jesus says, "I am the resurrection and the life." That was it, more or less.

I felt so sorry for those present, both mourners and onlookers, for having to hear such a soporific and (for a Christian) dishonest speech. It really gave nothing more than passing mention to Jesus, in whom alone there is eternal life. I actually feel urged to write to the pastor that, though the life of the deceased moved me, I'm sorry that *Jesus* was not honored at his grave – the Jesus who saves those who believe in him by grace alone, as he promises. Jesus said, "I am the resurrection and the life; whoever *believes* in me shall have life." *Not* "whoever has led a good life," though that's how this talk made it sound.

I'd really like to do this, but I won't. One, I don't know whether it's biblical for a young woman to speak out publicly; two, I'm the daughter of my parents, and I know it would be most unpleasant for them; three, I don't know whether I'm called to say anything like this to a pastor I don't even know and whose attitude to Jesus I don't really know either. On the other hand, I think it might at least cause him to reflect!

I believe I now know the great fault I constantly commit. I am concerned far too much with myself and with my sinful nature, instead of with Jesus. "Mine eyes always look to the Lord. He will draw my foot out of the net." That's how it should be. I have done what you advised: asked Jesus to show me everything I need to let go of, everything that prevents me from being filled with his Spirit, and I have promised to give it up – to sacrifice it for him. Just one thing: I've often promised him more in my prayers than I've actually kept to. Now I've asked him to guide me only by his Spirit. I'll give you an example. You know that we promised him to give up everything, including your and my honor, and to acknowledge his honor alone. That's how it has to be. But it's sometimes very hard, especially when you are praised. I felt this earlier but wasn't honest about it to God. I wanted to be honest, certainly, but don't believe I was. The strength to conquer such things comes only from faith.

You know, it's hard to write about this sort of thing, but I'm doing it anyway because I want us to help each other to blessedness, and I need you to pray for me. Besides, I think it's good to tell you *everything* so that you don't overestimate me. And if the Lord shows me more, I'll write about that too. You won't love me the less for it, I know, even if there are worse things to tell.

There's something else that bothers me. We recently discussed Colossians 3 – that we have died and risen with Jesus and have done away with everything and are reborn. It isn't like that with me. Since my conversion I've only recognized *little by little* all the sin in my heart. *Not* all at once. Am I then converted, but perhaps not yet reborn? I'm certainly determined to give up everything that doesn't come from Jesus. But I often wonder whether I'm really reborn. Of course, that's looking at myself again and not to Jesus, so that's wrong in itself. Jesus says, "Whoever believes in me will never see death." I do believe. Am I reborn, then? No matter what, I know I *want* to live completely according to Jesus' spirit and purpose.

I'm glad to have written everything to you now so that you can pray for me. I need so much help, also from Jesus.

On Saturday while I was with Lucia Franke, Olga went to Else Köhler's, though she wasn't invited to come in. I'm going to try once more tomorrow. I want to ask her directly whether she loves Jesus and wants to live for him – something like that. May God give me wisdom and a powerful witness.

I'd better close. I pray for you constantly and love you endlessly,

yours loyally, Emmy

Breslau
June 12, 1907

Matthew 5:12: "Rejoice and be glad, because great is your reward in heaven, for in the same way they persecuted the prophets who were before you."

Luke 6:23: "Rejoice in that day and leap for joy, because great is your reward in heaven. For that is how their fathers treated the prophets."

Philippians 4:4: "Rejoice in the Lord always. I will say it again: Rejoice!"

My glorious bride,

Your letters are steadily deeper and richer in content. Your fiftieth letter in particular was a great blessing and (what is especially important to me) gave me a deep glimpse into your heart, which I love with my whole soul. I rejoice over the initiation of the next fifty!

You're right: the most important thing is to look only to Jesus. Hebrews 12:2: "Let us fix our eyes on Jesus, the author and perfecter of our faith, who for the joy set before him endured the cross, scorning its shame, and sat down at the right hand of the throne of God." He who has given us our life of faith also completes it, as the crucified and exalted one. You'll find the same struggle you described in my own poems from 1905 (often rather strongly expressed) – how an oppressive awareness of sin can be completely overcome through looking to the cross. We'll read Luke 7:47 tomorrow. Even our sin can make Jesus greater and more glorious to us if only we look away from it, *to him.* See verse 50: "You shall go in peace." Not in reproaches of conscience – that is done away with.

Emmy, you *are* reborn, because you have life from God and you have Jesus. You love the Word and your brothers, etc. Never let the devil take that away from you. He who is converted is reborn. See Colossians 3:3: "For you died, and your life is now hidden with Christ in God." That describes my and your life, Emmy. But also read what the apostle Paul writes to the *same* people in verses 5–11. How much of the old nature must still be put aside before Christ is all in all! Renewal does not imply completion; rebirth is only the beginning of purification. It is normal to recognize more and more what is bad in us. So put it aside through Christ and keep moving forward.

As for praise: I've pondered it a great deal. I think it's all right for me to rejoice when you're praised, because I love you and want Jesus to be glorified through you. Look, if something good is said about me you need only think (if the good is really true): "Praise Jesus for blessing him," or "It's all from Jesus," or

"That's how a disciple of Jesus should be," or "He doesn't get that from himself. If only Jesus had more followers in whom he could do this. He really wants it for everyone." Finally, remember this, "Without Jesus he, too, would be nothing."

Yes, God and Jesus are honored by every being who allows him to work within, and we should rejoice about this. See Romans 1:8: "First, I thank my God through Jesus Christ for all of you, because your faith is being reported all over the world"; and 1 Thessalonians 1:8: "The Lord's message rang out from you not only in Macedonia and Achaia – your faith in God has become known everywhere. Therefore we do not need to say anything about it." Should the person concerned be the one we love most of all, then we should rejoice all the more. This, my beloved, is how I unite total love for Jesus with total love for you; and joy in Jesus with joy in you! Will you keep it this way with me, too? Oh, that we both might glorify him alone!

Happy in these thoughts,
your Ebbo

Halle
June 15, 1907

My Ebbo,

I just returned from a bible class at Frau Dr. Schulze's with Else. We spoke about Romans 1. I'm glad we're going through the Letter to the Romans, as I find it rather difficult.

Unfortunately I'm rather depressed today. I wasn't very nice to Frau Baehr after she questioned my stand on baptism the other day. I don't think I've died with Christ after all, or else I wouldn't be able to feel the least bitterness toward anyone, especially toward another believer who stands so firmly above me. It distresses me, and I have asked Jesus to master me more completely. I really don't want to be anything in human eyes, though, so it's probably good that other Christians don't always understand me. Maybe it will make me less bound to worry about other people's opinions, at least as regards the matter of baptism. The freer we are from human considerations, the more firmly will we be bound to Jesus – and he always understands us with our weaknesses.

I am so happy for the flowers (they are delightful!) and the writings you sent this morning. Your article in the *Alliance News* is very clear. I especially like what you write about Jesus and about the word of God. Yes, I will also pray that many, many students decide completely for him, so that they may be happy through him and work for him.

I'm looking forward to your next letter. Mama is surprised that we have so much to write about. She says she can't understand it at all. If she only knew! Greet your dear parents, and Betty, very warmly.

A thousand kisses,
your faithful Emmy

Breslau
June 16, 1907

Emmy, dear heart,

To begin with, I'm concerned about your health. I'm glad that you go out often on walks. Go on doing this and enjoying God's nature. But are you eating enough and sleeping properly? Maybe you're reading and writing too much. I'd happily do without your daily letters if they're a strain to write. Do you hear me, my love? The very best service you can do for me is to stay healthy and happy!

Which brings me to a deeper point. I think you brood too much and look into yourself much too often. Today's poem will tell you what I mean. You must hold more firmly to what we've talked about before – about how nothing but looking toward Jesus gives deliverance and certainty. Clearly, we must put up a determined fight against every sinful impulse, and we can't do this earnestly enough, but, my little dove, you mustn't remain downcast. If you've recognized something evil in yourself, or fallen in any way, *turn immediately to Jesus.* For when we come to Jesus and turn our backs on our sins, whether old ones or ones we've just committed, what happens? We're not thrust out but are drawn to his heart, as his own, and are filled with forgiveness, strength, and joy, so that we can rise again with praise and thanks. Romans 5:1–2. There *is* peace in faith and through our access to grace. Hallelujah! Here are just a few passages from Romans about joy:

15:13 May God fill you with pure joy and peace.

15:6 Praise God with one mind and voice.

15:7 Christ has accepted you to God's honor.
15:9 I will honor you and sing praises to your name.
15:10 Rejoice, all you nations.
15:11 Praise the Lord and glorify him.
12:15 Rejoice with those who rejoice – also in the innocent little joys of life.
12:12 Be joyful in your expectation of Jesus.

Isn't chapter 8 pure joy? Verse one says there's no longer any condemnation for those who are in Christ Jesus. O Emmy, don't we have pure cause for jubilation? There should be nothing but joy in us. In what we read from Luke today, too, it said we should rejoice that our names are inscribed and that we are saved. Can Satan or our sin or people ever take this joy away from us? No, they cannot. See John 16:22: "You will rejoice, and no one will take away your joy."

I want you to be joyful and happy always. There are so few Christians who are like that, because most of them don't understand the victory that comes from looking to Christ. Instead they keep looking inside themselves. That's the wretched life of Romans 7:7–24, a Christianity by law. Compare chapters 6 and 8.

Now to some particulars. It certainly hurts that you were mean to Frau Baehr – after all, she was an instrument of your conversion and a help in our engagement. But that's how we humans are. May it humble us and drive us to Jesus. He has forgiven you already. However, in keeping with Matthew 5:23–24, I would, if I were in your shoes, ask her forgiveness for this. "Therefore, if you are offering your gift at the altar and there remember that your brother has something against you, leave your gift there in front of the altar. First go and be reconciled to your brother; then come and offer your gift." At the same time tell her that her trust is very important to you, because you love her so much. Tell her that her comments were especially hurting to you because she misunderstood us. All we want is Jesus. I think that should resolve the problem (along with prayer, of course).

Why not go to Frau Baehr now and then to talk over things like your questions regarding the Letter to the Romans, just to show her your love and gratitude? I think you'll gain a lot from it.

Your Papa never wrote to me about the Anabaptists. If you think it's appropriate, give him the clipping of my article. Why did he only respond to the photograph and not my letter? Do you think there was something that displeased him, or did he just forget?

You're right in saying, "I feel myself to be so unworthy, yet that's when Jesus can do something."

It's splendid that your mother is reading the Bible with Else. I'm really very happy about that and have thanked Jesus for it. We must pray and believe. Jesus works miracles.

About me: I'm not completely happy about my studies. I ought to be moving along much more briskly. In part, I wasn't concentrated enough. And maybe I wrote too often to you. In spite of this, the Lord has blessed me and given me strength, which I'm thankful for. I've worked through Romans quite thoroughly, so that on Monday I'll only need to review it. Emmy, Romans is magnificent! I wish I could show you the clear, deep, glorious range of its thoughts. But we'll get to that later, my bride. Apart from that, I've gone through Luke as far as chapter 9 (vocabulary, translation, arrangement, memorization) and reviewed the other Gospels along with it. I've also worked a little on the Psalms. More significantly, I spent time studying the origin of the Gospels, etc.

My knee injury isn't worth mentioning. I just skinned it, and it's understandable that it hasn't healed more quickly, since I've kept walking and cycling.

I had a number of important experiences this week – the first, deeply shattering. I found out that a student who's been a *close* acquaintance of mine since 1903 committed suicide. He had a special devotion to me that I tried to divert, away from myself and toward Jesus. After I left school, other believers looked out for him. At times he could be quite resolute and fiery (possibly in emulation), but at other times he was full of doubts and disbelief. At the end he was dishonest, defiant, and arrogant. He suffered from a severe ear ailment, and was loyally cared for until the last, but he himself never became completely truthful and clear. That brought judgment on him. Was he ever converted? He *could* have been. Jesus was *often* very close to him, and yet he didn't want it! His life reminds me of Matthew 23:37: "O Jerusalem, Jerusalem, you who kill the prophets and stone those sent to you, how often I have longed to gather your children together, as a hen gathers her chicks under her wings, but you were not willing." Truth brings about decision: to the right *and* to the left, life *and* death!

In light of this event, I invited another student for a talk. Because of a strict, somewhat ascetic upbringing by born-again parents, he, too, has a tendency to dishonesty and a warped conscience. We spent about two blessed hours together in talk and prayer, and he said he felt it most important not to heed other people or feelings and ideas, but to heed Christ alone, in plain obedience to his word and simple trust in his promises. May Jesus bless him!

I still want to write down two interesting engagement stories. Several years ago, Betty made an unspoken pledge of love to Martin Streetz, a synod member's son, who in turn gave her an unmistakable avowal of his love, though he also never expressed it directly. Eventually he told our brother Hermann about it, and Hermann gave him to understand, in his distinguished, reserved way (just like Hermann!), that Martin ought first to finish his exams. So Betty waited about two years, during which Martin never made an appearance. (I myself was never in favor of it and had expressed this energetically.)

Now picture this: Betty and Mama are invited to a tea party at his parents' house, and in comes Martin. (They had no idea that he would be there.) "So *you're* here, Herr Streetz," says Mama rather coolly. "Of course he's here!" says his mother, "And this is his fiancée." And she introduces a very nice young woman to whom he'd become engaged that same day! Betty had fought the thing through long before, since Martin had never shown any loyalty to her. But it was still a blow, though at the same time a healing solution. Again, I had long deplored the despicable sluggishness of the man, so I took the opportunity to speak again very seriously with Betty. But I had little visible success.

Then today a born-again university student asked me for a chance to talk, and told me about his engagement. His fiancée is a fine, upright, believing woman, but he's been going through the most terrible torment over the last weeks. He fears he'll lose his sanity if it continues. In essence, he has grave doubts as to whether he and she are suited to each other, and because of this, his love for her has ebbed. It's the same with her: both think they are unworthy of the other, and because of this they have come close to dissolving their engagement. I told the young man quite decisively that I saw no obstacle from God here and that it would thus be a terrible sin for him to break off the engagement. I told him his task was to support and encourage his fiancée instead of making things more difficult for her, and that he would find strength for this in Jesus. I said all this in love, and he was grateful, and determined to write to her immediately about it. I am so thankful to Jesus that I was allowed to help someone in this way. Emmy, my love, how mercifully *we* are being led!

On another topic: I have been having serious doubts about my baptism theory over the last days and am feeling a strong inclination in favor of believers' baptism. This is not because of a particular passage, but because of a difficult question. How can one imagine the strictly separated body of *believers* that Jesus and the apostles established if the practice of baptism is to be extended in the sense that I formerly believed? Isn't this extension actually a defection from original Christianity? Since none of my explanations gave compelling proof *for* infant baptism, my position has been shaken, if not taken by storm. In fact, I'm quite unclear about the matter and am searching again. I feel almost convinced about baptism of believers. It came to me in prayer. I had read, "Woe to them that seek to extinguish the light," and said, "Lord, I never want to extinguish or divert it. Show me what you will. I will follow the light." It was then that a sudden insight, or so it seemed, came to me: "You have quenched the light of understanding with regard to the question of baptism – even if without wanting to."

Dear Emmy, all this is still unclear. Perhaps I am in error. But one thing is certain: I must (in August) test this issue very thoroughly, and I'm more determined than ever to obey God, with no evasion. I haven't spoken with *anyone* about this, nor do I want to at this point. Such a matter must be ripe before it's spoken about, or things will go wrong, and this may take a long time. We'll come to agreement with the Lord first, and only then act, no matter what.

But now I must close, my beloved. The Lord protect you. I'm so happy in him, and in you, and full of joy and peace.

Your faithful Ebbo

Testing

Focused as they were on the question of baptism, Eberhard and Emmy nontheless concerned themselves, in their letters, with the inner well-being of family members and friends. Feeling that Eberhard's youngest sister, Hannah, was compromising her faith, Emmy wrote to her that anything not done for Jesus' sake should be renounced. Eberhard in turn thanked Emmy for writing, but cautioned her as well: "Your viewpoint is quite right. Just be careful. To do everything wholly and solely for Jesus means much more than to limit one's sphere of activity in an ascetic way." Further clarifying his point, he said that it meant immersing oneself in modern society with all it has to offer, and "working it through" in such a way that Jesus alone would be glorified. He concluded, with regard to his sister, "She ought to realize that she is in the world to win souls for Jesus and to bring as many hearts as possible to him. Anything that contradicts this goal must be resolutely rejected."

Halle
June 25, 1907

My Ebbo,

Your letter yesterday made me immensely happy. I still don't have a definite position on baptism, though one thing I do know is that I personally didn't get *anything* out of my being baptized as a baby. I don't feel the slightest blessing in it. I came to God through my conversion, not through baptism.

Next Friday afternoon at 3:30 quite a number are going to be baptized: the Sallwürks, Frau Vogler, the Siewerts, Herr Zornow, a deaconess, Dönitz, and several from out of town as well. Else is praying constantly that she, too, can be baptized. Shall I too? Is it right, do you think? At times I think I should, but then again I *don't.* I've heard of people who have been baptized four or five times! Of course it's wrong to discuss such a question with flesh and blood; one ought to come to one's own recognition and then simply act. So if God clearly shows me that I should be baptized, I will definitely dare it. I know I'll be thrown out of the house if I do, but that isn't going to stop me.

With regard to Hannah, it moves me that she wants to be whole. You're right in cautioning me on my point of view. But Ebbo, I would be lying if I said, for example, "Now I'll go for a walk – for Jesus' sake." It's true that I'd still be completely at his disposal. If I head out toward Peissnitz Island, I still try to pay attention to whether he wants me to be doing something else, perhaps meeting other people. I try to let myself be led by him in every area. Yet if I said that I did everything directly *for* Jesus, I wouldn't be able to do anything but pray and save souls. And of course I also do other things, like sleeping or talking with unconverted people like my parents, without always speaking about Jesus. Indirectly I may be doing it for Jesus, but not directly. It would be self-delusion to think otherwise. Each morning I pray, "Lord, the day belongs to you. Lead me together with those through whom you can bless me or others; I am at your disposal." Another example: when we were in Breslau and went walking or boating, we were with Jesus, but we didn't do it *for* Jesus. We simply rejoiced in him. How do you see this?

Copying your poems isn't going very fast, but you'll get them soon. I think your latest one is wonderful. One other thing is that yesterday I realized I'd told a lie quite a long time ago to the matron I was working for at Salzwedel. Do you think Jesus would want me to put this in order, and by writing or in person? Lying has always been something I have hated, and yet without Jesus there is no truth. He is the truth. Everything else is illusion. Pray about what I should do.

But I must close. I still have ironing to do. Loving you endlessly,

your Emmy

Emmy knew how much her parents worried that she and Eberhard were influencing her sisters with their "unhealthy" brand of Christianity. Not wishing to aggravate tensions at home, she accepted an invitation to leave home for a few weeks and move in with the Freybes, family friends in Stappenbeck who needed a nanny for their children for the latter half of July. While Eberhard had no objections to the intended visit, he discerned ulterior motives on the part of Emmy's parents: "Incidentally, I have the impression your parents hope the Freybes will have a mitigating or softening effect on your Christianity. It's true that people like them – earnest, Christian-thinking people – are the very ones who often dampen the Spirit the most. Compromise is more difficult to see than outright rejection." Meanwhile, in Halle, the revivalists were growing increasingly divided over the issue of baptism, and emotions were running high.

Breslau
June 26, 1907

Psalm 150:6: "Let everything that has breath praise the Lord. Praise the Lord!"

My dearest Emmy,

My heart is full of joy, praise, and thanks – for our mighty Lord and for you, my glorious bride, the greatest gift he has given me!

Your letter requires a detailed answer, but today I can only answer fragmentarily, so you'll have to wait for my Sunday letter for a more thorough response.

Emmy's parents, Heinrich and Monika von Hollander, in Riga, ca. 1885

The deep split over the issue of baptism clearly originated with the Enemy. *Please* try, through Frau Baehr, to heal this wound in Halle. Read John 17: "That all of them may be one."

In regard to baptism, stand firm in the peace of Jesus. Don't press the Lord for an answer. His silence is an answer, too: a "No" for now. I believe the atmosphere in Halle is in any case working on you too strongly for you to be able to decide calmly and objectively. So wait, in faith and in dedication.

I consider indirect action for Jesus every bit as important as direct action, as long as the latter is there. If you didn't sleep or go for walks, etc., you'd be sinning against your body and making yourself unusable for Jesus' service. So you *are* doing these things for him. And if you talked with your parents only about Jesus, conversion, the Bible, etc., you'd have no access to their hearts whatsoever after a few days. Your responses to their interests, joys, and sorrows is therefore the most necessary and most important service you can do for them. Again, you are doing it for Jesus. In the same vein, I believe our boat rides and walks also served him. (The automobile ride, unfortunately, did *not,* because of my rashness. It has caused me many misgivings.) It follows that my studies are entirely for Jesus too. If I chose to drop them so as to save souls without interruption, I would in truth be acting *against* him.

My studies are going forward smoothly, though I still have a terrific amount to write. Oh, if only I had you with me, my beloved heart! But I'm happy for the Lord's leading. A number of times during the last days I was full of such impatient longing for you that he really had to purify me. Now I am much happier. *Jesus' leading is always best.*

Your Eberhard

Halle
June 29, 1907

Ebbo, my dearest beloved,

Today I didn't go to bible class or even for a walk, as Mama didn't want to let me out. In the evening, though, Else and I went to Brother Stenzel's, where we had a short bible study. He told us lots about yesterday's baptism, which took place at Cämern in a secluded little wood. What's really wonderful is that while they were there, a big rainbow appeared in the sky. Genesis 9:13: "I have set my rainbow in the clouds, and it will be the sign of the covenant between me and the earth."

It seems many in the movement are faulting Frau Dr. Schulze and us for not being present. Frau Dr. Schulze is against believers' baptism and has been misunderstood a great deal on account of it. But you know, my Ebbo, I'm not sure whether that's right. I think some of the baptizers are rather over-excited. I noticed it two evenings ago when Frau Siewert said that she was so happy, after being baptized, that it was like Christmas and that she felt like climbing a pole for joy. And Else kept saying, "Pray that I'll be allowed to be baptized. Pray that my legs be cut off and my eyes cut out, if it helps me to come to baptism." I said I considered it a sin to say something like that for the sake of baptism. God will bring it about if he wants to. I was apparently not understood, however. O Ebbo, if we're ever baptized, let's ask for a holy quietness, a holy peace beforehand. I find all this excitement awful! Of course I can understand people's happiness in being able to carry out the will of God as they have recognized it. Maybe it really is joy in the Holy Spirit. It's making me think.

But there's something else I've been wondering about. Will only those who are baptized be raptured? Are they the only ones who will belong to the Bride – the church? Have you ever thought about that? Revelation 14:1 says they had a sign on their forehead. Is it baptism?

I'm looking forward tremendously to your next letter. And because it's the 29th today, I keep thinking of March 29. How happy we are! Ephesians 1:14: "...who is a deposit guaranteeing our inheritance until the redemption of those who are God's possession – to the praise of his glory." Psalm 34.

I must close since we're eating soon.

In faithful love in Jesus,
your bride

Breslau
June 29–30, 1907

My Emmy,

I've just returned from a powerfully blessed Salvation Army meeting. The major allowed me to lead the meeting, and I was greeted with loud hallelujahs and beaming faces by the many members who came. After we prayed several times on our knees and I told them something about Halle and about all of you (without mentioning names), I spoke in the strength of the Spirit, whom I had received in prayer from the Lord, about Romans 6:11–13. The meeting was extremely moving – practically only converted people were there. Many confessed to unfaithfulness, and some broke down sobbing violently. In general, the spirit of prayer took hold most forcefully of every heart. Emmy, how glorious it is that Jesus has again heard and used his most worthless servant! I've seldom experienced anything like it.

I myself was deeply moved but tried to conduct the meeting in quiet confidence. Many others became very excited, in Salvation Army fashion, so I admonished them to peace and silence before God. The main thing, however, is that God's spirit clearly and sharply revealed sin in the most varied and hidden forms, and almost all the dear souls present took hold of full salvation in Jesus. May Jesus preserve their blessedness! I know he will. You know, I love the Salvation Army so much that sometimes I wish I could work there more. But I can do it only as an exception.

Your sweet letters, my beloved, make me very happy! Every one has enormous value – my Bible and your letters are the most precious things I own.

Baptism seems to concern you a great deal, my love. Of course it's not the sign mentioned in Revelation 14:1. All who overcome through the Word, that is, all who are reborn and love the Word in faith and obedience, according to their understanding, receive the name of God on their foreheads. Revelation 3:7–12. No particular condition is given for the rapture, except that of being in Christ. See 1 Thessalonians 4:16–17: "For the Lord himself will come down from heaven, with a loud command, with the voice of the archangel and with the trumpet call of God, and the dead in Christ will rise first. After that, we who are still alive and are left will be caught up together with them in the clouds to meet the Lord in the air. And so we will be with the Lord forever."

The agitation over baptism doesn't seem right to me. It cannot be of the Holy Spirit. Else's excited protestations, too, are superfluous, senseless, and wrong, and thus not of the Holy Spirit either. If God wants to do something, he will do it. I thought Else had become calmer. She had appeared to. It won't go well for her unless she takes a clear attitude to this unhealthy excitement.

My position with regard to baptism is clearer since yesterday. I was stimulated by the text you sent, which I've put up over my desk. I also drafted the enclosed poem, thinking of our possible baptism and of the persecutions prophesied in the end times. Afterward I rode to a quiet wood to reflect and pray. I want to stress three points:

1. Under all circumstances, I will do only the clearly recognized will of God.
2. I will do nothing except what I am convinced of after examining it from all sides.
3. I will not go forward with anything that I can't clearly verify as biblical, and therefore am unable to justify with precision to anyone.

My impression is that there are three things I need to do in the near future:

1. Search the New Testament and history in general for references to the baptism question.
2. Have myself baptized *if* my present inclination toward baptism of believers can be shown to be biblical. I will do this as soon as I am sure that my position is firm scientifically; that is, according to the Bible and to history.

3. Publish three booklets – on the church, conversion, and baptism in early Christian times.

The practical outcome of this is such:

1. I feel I cannot be baptized at this point without sinning.
2. After my next two exams, I will devote my private study to the questions of the church and of baptism.
3. I'll probably be baptized in a few years. I can and will say nothing definite about this, however, before concluding my studies. Therefore we need to remain silent!

More about my work: If all goes well, I hope to be a candidate for a doctorate in theology in March 1909 (and also officially your bridegroom). At that point I'll immediately set to work publishing, within a year, the three above-mentioned booklets, which belong together inwardly and will be followed by others, perhaps according to the following plan:

I. The wholeness / purity of the original Christian church communities.
II. Conversion in original Christianity.
III. Early Christian baptism.
IV. The witness of the apostles.
V. The gifts of original Christianity.
VI. Early Christian organization.

As regards the step of baptism: I will only take it if I come to recognize its validity for believers on the basis of my own research. I myself must convince my critics that it's a calm, clearly reasoned conviction of the will of Jesus and the apostles that has brought me to such a step. Otherwise people will be quick to say, "First the Salvation Army and now baptism. He's always going to extremes! It's because of his temperament."

No, whatever I do, I want to do with complete conviction. It's clear to me that this way (i.e. a clear motive for every action) is the will of the Lord. If, through my studies, I should remain in my former conviction, that's okay. Then I'll prove the validity of *infant* baptism. Either way, I'll need to act calmly and objectively, without judging others and without pushing Jesus from the center. What I really wish, of course, is that you be baptized with me and not before me, *if the Lord leads it like that.* All this is, of course, only for you. Don't say anything to *anyone* for now.

Thank you immensely for copying out the poems. I was so happy to see them in your beloved handwriting. I'm just sorry I haven't received any of yours. Haven't you written any recently?

I love it when you tell me something that bothers you. Let's always tell each other everything, even if it's hard. That's the ideal relationship and the only right one, as far as I'm concerned.

Pray for me! Heat is harder to deal with than cold, and it's important that I go on working hard. On Monday morning I need to finish up with the Gospels and the Letters to the Corinthians (this week's work, and then on Monday we'll read Acts 1, right?). Next week I'll need a lot of time to prepare my sermon on Matthew 21:28–32, which I'm giving on July 13. It will be in two parts:

1. Christianity not as rest, but work.
2. The kingdom of God not as a matter of words, but of power. Not words, but action.

In the past week I've struggled a good deal inwardly: 1) I had to bring my passionate longing for you to the Lord again and again. I thank you for your loving words about this. Pray that I always remain happily peaceful in Jesus, whose leading is the best, for it will always give us certainty that our souls are completely one.

2) I've had serious worries at times when thinking of your and my beloved parents in the event that we should have ourselves baptized. I see this as a very grave matter and am extremely afraid, out of love to them. Pray that I hold firm in faith. He will not lead us into error, if we're sure to obey Jesus and the Bible alone! We don't want to obey inner voices and feelings, etc., but to stand on the Word, on scripture, as it reveals itself to us through thorough, obedient searching. John 15:10: "If you obey my commands, you will remain in my love, just as I have obeyed my Father's commands and remain in his love."

3) I've been concerned about those students who are unhappy that I don't go to their meetings more often. Because of this I won't be writing to you again until Thursday. I just won't have time on Wednesday.

4) You know how depressing the Lucia Franke business is to me. I've entrusted it to the Lord, and I know he will help the poor girl. But if only I'd been wiser and holier! I count myself guilty because of my carelessness. I would tell you more details, but the whole thing is repugnant to me. If only the matter were buried forever! If you must, you can tell Else about everything, including my behavior and thinking at the time. You know I have nothing to hide. But tell her only if you must.

In connection with this, I also want to tell you that I think (but am not totally sure) that there's another young woman who was interested in me. Her name is Käthe Gude, and I know her brothers well through a bible class we took together years ago. One of them is going to be, or already is, a naval officer. I was an instrument – the decisive one, I believe – of Käthe's conversion when we were together at a summer resort in the Riesengebirge. Because of her behavior toward me at that time, I felt she loved me more than just as a brother. Georg Herde seemed to have noticed the same, because when I told him of our engagement, he said, "I always thought you'd get engaged to Käthe Gude." That was unpleasant for me, since I never loved her – you know how I mean that – and kept my distance from her, though one time I accompanied her home, because it just turned out that way. I'm telling you all this only because I'd rather tell you too much than too little. Until now I'd never thought of it; it was never important to me. Please write to me what you think about all this.

5) It's been hard for me that my darling sister Clara doesn't understand my insistence on complete decisiveness. It's already sad that Betty is undecided, but it's much worse that Clara is still so involved in society, etc., although she does sometimes avoid it. She also admits that a tremendous amount of what goes on is unimportant and unproductive. What's missing in her, though, is wholehearted dedication to the service of Jesus Christ, and that's a deep pain to see. Let's pray that God becomes fully victorious in both our families!

O Emmy, I think you greatly overestimate me in your love! You don't know, for example, how dreadfully limp and cowardly I can be when I have not let myself be filled with Jesus' spirit. It's that way in everything – in my struggle with sin, untruthfulness, arrogance, laziness, and many other things. I've wanted to tell you this for a long time already. Pray and pray for me and help me, my strong, sweet little bride, to become a man who goes from victory to victory through Jesus!

Wanting to show you my whole weak self, and trusting you boundlessly in deepest earthly and heavenly love, I am yours from head to toe,

Ebbo

Breslau
July 3, 1907

1 Timothy 1:14: "The grace of our Lord was poured out on me abundantly, along with the faith and love that are in Christ Jesus."

Emmy, my happiness,

How I wish I could write you a truly joyous letter, since I pray above all that God may daily overwhelm you with joy and strength! You want, however, to share in everything, also the difficult things, and that's also right. It is because of this that our happiness is so deep: because it's honest through and through and doesn't conceal even what is most painful. I haven't experienced anything new – don't worry about that – it's old things that have been weighing me down in recent days.

Unfortunately my work has gone very poorly since Monday, and it didn't improve until today. One of the reasons for this was recalling all the details of the entire Lucia Franke situation. I've become terribly downcast thinking about it.

I've already told you so much about her that I feel terrible about coming back to it again and again. But on thinking it over now, the old struggles have become clearer to me, and I must write down my thoughts for you in detail immediately.

When I first got to know Lucia last summer, she impressed me with her quiet, determined Christianity. I didn't see her for a long time then, so I was glad when I suddenly got a card from her. She wrote to me repeatedly – so much so that Fritz Böhm immediately concluded she was madly in love. I met her next at an SCM meeting, at a discussion regarding the Young Women's Union. She was extraordinarily nice to me and asked for my assistance on a number of things, which I gladly gave.

Thus I was suddenly part of her family and was often invited to her parents' home along with Fritz Böhm. This was frequently embarrassing for us, since she wanted to spend time just with him, for discussion and prayer, and then just with me. I was foolish enough – wrong – to agree to it. In the meantime I was having severe inner struggles about the whole thing, since Fritz was trying to take away my innocence. Because I didn't know you, who infinitely exceed my highest hopes and prayers, I didn't have any idea what love is and persuaded myself at times, without really believing it, that I loved Lucia and that one day, years down the road, I might perhaps become engaged to her. (This is what has weighed on me most, though I already told you this at our engagement.) As a consequence, I became too deeply involved with her to give her an objective yes or no. I did strenuously maintain limits to our relationship: everything had the character of a mere friendship. But it's still very embarrassing how Fritz kept saying that I was in love with her, and that I put up with it.

Then, more and more frequently, there were hours when the whole thing became extremely distasteful to me, particularly when her conduct bordered on being pushy. That's when I began to wrestle more deeply and earnestly in prayer that God might free me completely from her. But then again there arose in me a feeling of sympathy that wouldn't allow me to make the break. At last, in January, I wrote her the letter I've mentioned to you before, where I made my feelings explicit. What was I to do, then, when she told me she didn't understand it? I withdrew from her company as much as possible and emphasized my happiness in her future plans to be a doctor in India. I insisted that we avoid every appearance of being engaged, since we were only friends and people so easily get the wrong idea. But the thing kept getting sadder and more oppressive. By then it had long since been clear to me that nothing in the way of engagement and marriage could ever be considered.

Since I met you, my glorious bride, I've come to see the matter more seriously. Though unwitting at the time, I now recognize more clearly my great wrong, which consisted chiefly in lacking energy to make a radical break with Lucia. It's all very dark and difficult for me. I always prayed to do what was right, but God permitted this to happen, perhaps to humble me and purify me.

Once I'm in Halle I can tell you even more, awful as the details are. You know, every thought of Fräulein Franke is a torment to me. I don't want to say that I hate her – that would be a sin – though I'm fighting a certain repugnance and anger, which I know Jesus will conquer. I actually wish many blessings on her. Yet merely seeing her would be terrible for me, perhaps also because of the temptation to have sympathy.

I ask you, my Emmy, to tell me your opinion on all this in detail as soon as you can, and to help me overcome *everything* that is wrong. I'd really never seen the matter so clearly until now. I feel terrible about distressing you with it now, but I have to for your sake. I'm unspeakably sad about this whole painful affair. Only when you're no longer burdened by this will I also be freed, and no sooner.

Pray, Emmy, that I may study more and do so more eagerly. Papa asked me today if my zeal was flagging somewhat, and I had no reply for him. Then both of my parents said we were corresponding too often (given my studies), and Mama said you must be the cause of it. It's not that any of this is very important to me, but on the other hand you always want to know about such things. It would be very hard for me if you wrote less, but if the *Lord* wants it of us, I'll agree to any restriction. At any rate, don't strain yourself writing to me. If you've worked too hard during the day and are tired out or sleepy, leave it.

Your extremely loving letter arrived just now and comforts me a great deal and makes me very happy! No one could imagine what a sweetheart you are! I'm especially glad that *you're* happy again. May God give you strength to overcome the contents of this letter soon; cast everything on the Lord in prayer, be joyful, and make me joyful too. The photo of you makes me immensely happy! I'm putting it in my wallet. The texts are splendid too. My love, on no account should you stay awake at night thinking things over. Nighttime is for sleeping. Discipline yourself. I will too – I also sometimes go to sleep very late because I'm thinking of you. Let us always pray before going to bed that God will give us the refreshment of uninterrupted sleep. But that's enough for now. Again, a thousand thanks for the great joy of your letter today.

Loving you with total devotion,
your Ebbo

Halle
July 4, 1907

My one and only Ebbo,

Today's letter drives me to prayer. What else can I say? You know, I think you're innocent in the matter. For my part, I consider Lucia Franke a thorough Christian (perhaps further along than I), but from what I know of her, I also believe that she is altogether tactless and lacks sensitivity in such things as relationships. I think it was totally unfitting for her to try to be alone with you. I'm not saying you shouldn't have prayed with her. In certain circumstances I might have done that, too, though never again, after this. I saw the same thing at the children's worship services with Pastor Lichtenstern (who was transferred because he was "too serious" and "too Christian" for Pastor Knuth). Imagine how the ladies swarmed around *him,* even going to his private home to discuss inner matters! I saw some pretty shocking things there. Olga warned him at that time, when he was at our house, but he wouldn't listen. Then – imagine this – when he left the parish, several ladies went to the consistory claiming that he'd "deceived" them, and the daughter of one washerwoman even claimed he had asked her to marry him. (That's impossible of course, and no one will ever believe her.)

But to your concern: Ebbo, I believe many young women have been made unhappy by similar things. I do think you shouldn't have gone to her house as much as you did, even if you believed at times that you loved her. I myself don't understand it, but you know that most women so quickly jump to conclusions. I've always been told that I don't understand such matters. Well, I'm thankful to God for it. But there *must* have been Christian women Lucia knows with whom she could have talked things over. It's hard to believe she didn't realize at all how unfittingly she was behaving! I'm very sad that you're fighting aversion or anger. I pray you'll conquer those feelings. We should rather be praying for her that she overcomes her false love for you, becomes more sensitive, and gives everything over to Jesus. That's what we both want to do in this matter so that we can be completely happy again. Because of course he wants us to be happy – that's why he led us together. I also want you to be fully at peace again, Ebbo. Listen, Jesus knows that you didn't want to do any wrong, only what *he* wanted, and that's what both of us want now too. I don't believe you can do anything more, now, than give the matter over to Jesus and then be happy again.

Now to the other thing I want to tell you: I pray very often for your studies. This morning I was downcast, thinking that we might be writing too often. Certainly it's only in the last week that you've written to me so often, and there was some particular reason each time. But perhaps I'm writing to you too often. Maybe it would be better if I only wrote three times a week? Next week I'll be at the Freybes, so I won't be able to write as often anyway. And later, when I'm somewhere else, it'll be all the more difficult. Tell your dear parents *that!* Surely it's all right for you to say that this week there was special reason to correspond.

This morning I was at Frau Dr. Schulze's. The fellowship was wonderful. I always learn a lot from her. Today I still have quite a bit to do, so I can't write any longer. Perhaps I'll go to the Alliance class this evening. I'd really like to. Pray that I'm given more strength! I pray for you and for Lucia Franke and for your studies and letter writing and everything. Be happy, Ebbo. I am happy in you, and in Jesus. I'll pray right now and tell him everything. Your last poem is *so* sad. I beg you: be happy!

I haven't copied all of your poems yet. I don't get around to it very often. (I'll send you mine when I can, though I only found a couple.) Pray also for what I am undertaking now – that I may go where he wants to have me!

In deep love and completely at one with you in prayer and in everything,

your Emmy

Breslau
July 4, 1907

My darling Emmy,

Your letter was again an overflowing source of joy for me! Yes, you're right; many times when I longed for you it wasn't from Jesus, and I will overcome this fully. You're also right, we can't do more than give thanks! But I won't be completely happy until I see (from your next letter) that you've overcome the contents of mine from yesterday, or at least that you're not finding it unbearable. If you are sad, so am I; if *you* are happy, then I will be too! Today I only have one thing to tell you: I have never yet loved one single person on earth except for you! Even my love for my family and best friends was a cloudy drop compared to the crystal-clear ocean of love I have for you. And the rest wasn't really love at all.

Emmy, you alone,
no other, do I love.

Emmy, for you
alone do I breathe.

Emmy, you alone –
my endless repose.

Emmy, together
we're the Savior's own.

Loving you more than ever in Jesus, your Ebbo

Halle
July 5, 1907

Ephesians 1:14: "...who is a deposit guaranteeing our inheritance until the redemption of those who are God's possession – to the praise of his glory."

Colossians 1:13: "For he has rescued us from the dominion of darkness and brought us into the kingdom of the Son he loves."

My Ebbo,

I actually wasn't going to write to you today, but I think you'll want to know that I'm completely happy again after receiving your letter today. I've given the whole thing over to Jesus and no longer feel the slightest burden from it. Ebbo, we ought to love Lucia Franke. She's really a very fine young woman, and she *does* want to follow Jesus. Perhaps she can't help her tactlessness. It's probably not right of me to say this, but I don't like your praying alone with any girl other than myself. If it's really necessary for her sake, or for Jesus, that's something else. If you consider it important, you will of course do it. But I don't like it at all.

Another thing: I really don't see anything wrong in writing each other so often. It is Jesus, after all, who has led us together so that we can help each other – and especially so that you can help me, since I don't have nearly as much wisdom as you have. I don't think our parents can understand this, however, so maybe it *is* better if I don't write too often, so that it doesn't upset them. Maybe it will be better for your studies too.

Yesterday I attended a wonderful Alliance meeting. The theme was Isaiah 53. Many confessed their sins in the prayer – you can imagine how moving that was. I also prayed. Normally I don't do this in such gatherings, but I was urged to. Else and Monika were with me, and the latter cried bitterly on the way home, though she wouldn't tell us why. When we got home there was great excitement again. It's actually always like that afterward.

Thinking of you always and praying for you,
your Emmy

Breslau
July 7, 1907

Acts 2:47: "They praised God with jubilation."

Emmy, you incomparably sweet thing,

I praise God with jubilation for his tremendous mercy and above all for your delightful letter. It wasn't right to torment myself with the fear that you might get the wrong idea about me and Lucia. But I've learned a great deal over these difficult days. I thought I was already being cautious, but now I will be even more so. After what we've been through, I don't believe Jesus could ever give a young man like me the task of praying alone with a young woman who isn't engaged to him. (I understand only now why in other movements of awakening and evangelization, men and boys are counseled only by men, and women and girls only by women, and I will make this rule my own.)

As you can imagine, it was hard to write you so much about Lucia Franke and Käthe Gude. Verbally it would have been much easier, but I'm glad I did it, because now I'm so free! I will always tell you everything of importance, whatever it may be, even if it's very hard. That's how we both want it to be, I am sure. Imagine, Mama told me today that she has reproached Papa for always telling her unpleasant things. Other men keep secrets, but I believe it's false love. Certainly, one doesn't need to bother one's partner with passing or quickly-overcome difficulties, but I beg you to share with me, unconditionally, everything that is a real burden, and I will require the same of myself.

You know, we can't look to the world for answers. There probably isn't one clear relationship in a thousand in the sense we mean it. Even among serious Christians we have been exceptionally blessed. This is becoming more and more obvious to me. My happiness is like a deep, clear ocean that can never be exhausted.

Thanks to the Lord, I don't have the slightest burden now and am again strong in his joy. Whatever comes, I know I will conquer, because Jesus and his Holy Spirit dwell in me. Even the little scenes between the others at home can in no way rob me of this peace.

In fact, the Lord has helped me so much that my parents even ask me to help make peace in family squabbles. It's most disagreeable for me as a son, of course, and I keep as far away as I can from all conflicts. But it's a testimony to Jesus that

I'm now being called on for this, whereas before, I was always being rebuked for causing nothing but dissension and controversy with my Christianity. Papa still gets annoyed about my "attitude" at times, but on the whole he is very nice to me. He himself prays a great deal – I often hear his rather complaining murmur. But as far as I can see, he doesn't receive any strength from praying. What a sad religion! How I praise God for having given me victory in Christ Jesus, so that I know the true joy of a happy life and of strength!

I'm planning to leave here on August 4. How long I will stay with you all I can't say yet. It will certainly be only a few days – maybe three, maybe a few more, as Jesus leads it. Perhaps Frau Baehr will ask me to hold some bible classes? I'd be glad to. Greet her very warmly. You can't give her all my poems, but you could give her one or another whose contents are meaningful for any Christian. If I had time, I'd be glad to copy something for her.

I must admit that your letters always occupy me tremendously, and to that extent they also affect my studies. Because of this it might perhaps be good after all to write less frequently. On the other hand, however, they are always a great stimulus and a real help for my work. And my good parents no longer seem so concerned about our frequent writing. Mama only said, "But you can't exhaust the whole of theology, or of love either." Therefore, darling, let's stick to our own system until the Lord gives us a different leading. Others can never completely understand. We really need no one else but the two of us for this – right?

Keep praying for me that it comes to the point where *everything* I do is for Jesus. And let's be thankful when he uncovers wounds and heals them. We should always ask him to show us our sins – also the ones we weren't aware of. If only I can become purer and more usable for Jesus, I want to bear even what is most painful with thanks and praise.

Already four years ago, these three verses by my Uncle Martin Kögel were of great value to me:

Holy pruning knife, cut deeply into me,
for I am still not yet as pure as I should be.

Holy pruning knife – see how I kiss thy blade?
You'll save my soul from death, and so I'm not afraid.

Holy pruning knife, let me be silent then.
If I need more, cut deeply once again!

Let's hold to this, Emmy, and remain pure for him at all costs.

These days my thoughts, besides being with you, have also been with the students in Halle a great deal. I've prayed for them a lot. One converted student wrote to another here, "The circle here (the SCM) has received the most powerful stimuli. People aren't all cut from the same cloth, dogmatically speaking, like those in Breslau. On the contrary, there's the greatest variety of individuals and therefore of views, though at the same time the living Christ *is* in the foreground. But compared to last semester, there will most likely be a setback. Arnold and von Gerdtell's enthusiasm has abated."

What do you think, Emmy? I have very mixed feelings about it. Please write me exactly how you think this might affect the circle in Halle. Read and discuss it with Frau Baehr too! The writer, Erich Schiller, is a quiet, diligent worker. He tries to serve Jesus in his way but isn't decisive enough to take a consistent stand, from what I can tell.

You know, when I came to Halle, there was unequalled confusion in the SCM. Remind me in August to tell you about it. True, God gave victory after victory through prayer and grace; he let the spirit of Jesus rule by driving back everything alien and unclear. We experienced wonderful, glorious things. But it wasn't I, nor von Gerdtell, nor anyone else. It was the Lord and his spirit.

Anything that might have come from *us* must die, the faster the better. Let us pray, Emmy, that the Lord's work may grow and deepen and become clearer among the students of Halle.

I'm all alone today at home, thinking of the heavenly hours when we were alone together, and I sat at your feet by the piano! Emmy, you'll gradually come to see what a wretched person I am. But Jesus is victor! Hallelujah forever!

I asked Ludwig Treutler to sing, "After the storm we'll pass safely through the waves" for me! It made me so happy, and I thought of you and myself and Jesus! My dear, sweet Emmy, I've prayed so hard that you might be really happy and joyful again and that you really get plenty of rest and sleep. That should be possible now, right? It's natural to have struggles, but it's also important to be innocently joyful, and you do that so marvelously.

I wish Monika would talk with somebody. I'd also like to hear whether Heinz's conversion is real. Greet everyone very warmly, especially your dear parents. Let's continue to pray and have faith for them. And what are the sweet children doing?

I might go to the tent mission still today. I'm only anxious about getting to bed late because of work tomorrow. It's quite far south, three-quarters of an hour away, but I have a great longing for God's word.

What did you think of my plan for the books on early Christianity? I'm very inspired about it.

Beloved, I'm so worried about your health! Please be peaceful and stay strong in the peace of Jesus! Psalm 68:20: "Our God is a God who saves; from the Sovereign Lord comes escape from death."

I kiss you as his possession and belong to you alone in fullest happiness,

Ebbo

Halle
July 8, 1907

My Ebbo,

Your long letter today made me very happy again. I don't have much time to write today.

I agree with you that telling each other everything is absolutely necessary. I think it's disgraceful when engaged couples lie to each other, and it often happens. We'll never do that!

I'm going to Frau Baehr's this afternoon to discuss all sorts of things, and I'll also tell her that you'd be glad to hold bible classes. There will be nasty scenes at home if you have them at Frau Baehr's, but we can avoid that by having them somewhere else. I'll discuss it with Frau Baehr.

I'll also talk with her about the SCM. I don't know, but I have the feeling the movement is slowing down. Maybe that's because not everybody is of the same stamp dogmatically and all views are valid, for example, that God's word is *in* the Bible, and *not the Bible*. It also seems to me that things have become quieter, as if the awakening is coming to a standstill. I could be wrong about that though. I'm praying constantly that his Spirit is not stopped.

I consider Heinz's conversion very unclear; I do not notice any change. I use every opportunity to speak with him about Jesus.

I think your plan with the books is fine. Such books about original Christianity are just what we lack.

One other thing: I was told in confidence yesterday by Pastor Westerhof that Fräulein von Nostiz has brought indescribable confusion and discord here in Halle within the movement, especially in regard to baptism. It's also said she's tried to introduce foot washing. Then I heard from Lucia Franke that one of the newly baptized people was very unhappy with herself because she had gotten baptized only because Fräulein von Nostiz persuaded her to. Apparently she tried to convince two other young women for two hours in the little birch wood and said there would be judgment upon them if they didn't get baptized! She's also tried with Frau Dr. Schulze, Monika, and others. If no uniting takes place, there's likely to be a split between those for and those against adult baptism. Such a rift between Christians is extremely sad. I and others are trying everything possible to restore unity.

O Ebbo, pray that they all may be united again under the cross. Instead of bringing others to Jesus they are wasting a lot of time in quarrelling. I must close now.

In warmest love, happy in Jesus and in you,
your Emmy

Breslau
July 14, 1907

Psalm 16:11: "You have made known to me the path of life; you will fill me with joy in your presence, with eternal pleasures at your right hand."

My dear Emmy,

I can imagine you sitting happily together with the dear Freybes and their little ones. Maybe you're having lunch now and telling them many wonderful things about Jesus' glorious leading. I am very happy, Emmychen, that you are there.

I'm glad that you have all been making efforts to prevent the painful division in Halle. I'm asking for strength from the Lord to heal this wound in the body of Christ. You'll most likely have fewer upsets now that you're in Stappenbeck. I am very glad about that. I pray that you'll be able to sleep well too.

When I come to Halle, I wish very much, Emmy, that you would tell me more about the years you worked as a nurse. You've hardly told me anything. It moved me to hear that you've already been with twenty to thirty people when they died. Last summer when I was attending the tent mission, I also had a deeply shattering impression of how lost and far away from God men are! O Emmy, in Germany alone there is so terribly much to do! Thousands die of thirst without a drop of living water! And there are even more outside of Germany, where there is no established church to bring God's word to the masses. I myself would gladly go out. I'm only worried that I'm a little too old. By the time I would finish preparing in areas like learning the language, years will have gone by, and I want to use my whole strength in saving souls and in building up his kingdom. But God is the one who leads us.

Finney's talks are very incisive. Sharp self-examination is the best preparation for new blessings, assuming that one keeps his eyes directed to *Jesus.* I wish you, my little dove, would find something different to read for now, something that would lead you more directly to joyful faith. Finney can do that, but you should stop reading him if he diverts your eyes from Jesus. If you understand him completely *in Jesus,* you will gain enormously. O Emmy, how much more wonderful it will be when we can read, pray, and think through everything together.

I am always very close to you, my love!
your faithful Ebbo

Many warm greetings from Papa, Mama, and Betty.
Notice that I am very happy *in Jesus!*

Emmy stayed in Stappenbeck until July 29. The Halle revival, and Emmy's involvement in it, was a frequent topic at the Freybes' table and elsewhere, as Pastor Freybe would not give up trying to turn the "naïve" young woman back to the sober Christianity of the established church. But Emmy would not yield.

Stappenbeck
July 20, 1907

My Ebbo,

Yesterday I received your letter and also a very nice one from Clara. I can't write in peace, since little one-year-old Renate is sitting next to me and is extremely restless. She wants to be entertained all the time.

On Monday I will probably go to Salzwedel, but it's still indefinite. This morning I received the magazine and the article "For Infant Baptism" from you. I haven't managed to read it yet. Besides that, I was glad to receive a card from Hermann and Käthe.

You wouldn't believe how difficult it is to write a letter when you're trying to take care of a child! But now I'm finally alone for a moment.

There's something I want to tell you about. On my way here I overheard a very animated discussion between a deaconess, two Red Cross sisters, and two ladies who were traveling with me. One of them (I think she's a children's nurse) told her life story in tears. She was dreadfully unhappy – she's an orphan who's been pushed back and forth by strangers, and she's never found contentment anywhere. I didn't really take part in the conversation, but I did tell her that one won't find satisfaction anywhere in the world – that peace can be found only in Jesus. When she got off the train, I asked her for her address, and she gave it to me. I want to write her and enclose a card with the bible text, "Behold, I stand at the door and knock," and invite her to come to Jesus. I'm earnestly praying for her too.

You know, Ebbo, it's nice here, but I wouldn't want to stay for months. The Freybes run around all day long and never finish. To them, Christianity means constantly chasing after things and carrying out even the smallest duties conscientiously. That may be true in a certain way. In Halle, I did wonder about the many housewives who never missed a meeting and often went to bible classes both afternoon and evening. I wondered if it wouldn't please the Lord more if they put their lives at home in order. I'll tell you in person about a few other doubts I have. But in general, don't you think every Christian needs time for quiet – for Jesus and his word – at least once a day, in addition to fellowship with other Christians?

I need your prayers. I may already return home next week. Frau Hachtmann is coming to Halle then and wants to talk with me. Her husband is a pastor and an acquaintance of a friend of mine, and they need temporary help in their household in Brumby.

But I need to close. The little one is drinking her bottle. I hope she'll go to sleep, or else I'll soon have to pick her up again.

Kissing you with deep love,
your bride

Oh, how I look forward to seeing you!

Breslau
July 21, 1907

My delightful bride,

At this moment my only wish is that you be just as happy as I am. The reason is not a new one. It is *Jesus* and *you!*

This week the Lord helped me especially in my work. I finished all the letters of Paul and will soon be finished with the Acts of the Apostles too. What shall we read next? Today we should be reading Acts 21, right? Didn't it strike you how their fellowship in prayer was completely free of shyness? Read for example Acts 21:5. The entire book of Acts is absolutely modern. In a thousand ways it portrays the original Christian character of our awakening movement.

But now to finish. Today Pastor Hänisch and a government construction engineer, a converted acquaintance of mine, are coming for coffee. God protect you, my love! I hope Renate lets you read this letter in peace.

your endlessly loving Eberhard

Remember me to the Freybes.

Changing Course

Eberhard spent most of August at an SCM conference in Wernigerode, where, to his surprise, he was nominated chairman of the meetings. Many students were converted at the conference, and Eberhard left encouraged, despite differences remaining within the movement over the issues of adult baptism and speaking in tongues. He returned to the University of Breslau at the beginning of September. Meanwhile, Emmy spent an uneventful month at home. The young couple met several times, both at a student conference in Blankenburg and in Halle, where the controversy over baptism was growing and causing a rift in the revival movement. Emmy was distressed by this: she felt all the talk threatened to displace Jesus. When in one letter she expressed her disquiet after an especially convinced proponent of adult baptism called her a corpse, since she had "died with Jesus, but not been buried and resurrected through baptism," Eberhard responded, "Listen, my little bird, do you consider me a corpse? I don't." Not surprisingly, she was glad for the chance to move, at least temporarily, to nearby Brumby in order to help in the home of Pastor Hachtmann and his wife.

Eberhard, 1907

Breslau
September 3, 1907

Emmy, my darling,

I really wanted to open this letter on a joyful note, so as to comfort and encourage you, but the fact is I'm still very sad. I just don't know how to deal with your long absence – you, whom I love so endlessly! I feel as though my heart were torn from my breast. But that's foolish and sinful. After all, you're still completely there, in my heart, and I am in yours.

I don't know what makes me sadder: the pain of our separation, or the sinful passion it's caused. Everything looks black in my present state of mind: the baptism question, the conflicts in the SCM, our family difficulties, my exams – everything.

But now, beloved Emmy, about two hours after having begun this letter, I can finally tell you I'm happy and calm again in Jesus, even if I'm not cheerful enough to be laughing. On the basis of God's word, I've accepted his forgiveness and help and given over everything wholly to him. The Lord's word is the sole source of strength for me in matters of faith and obedience, and I beg him to make me simple – truly and utterly simple – in regard to it. I need this so badly and *want* it. 1 Peter 1:24–25 has become vitally important to me, which is surely the Lord's doing: "All flesh is like grass, and all its glory is like the flowers of the field; the grass withers and the flowers fall, but the word of the Lord stands forever." If we stand completely in the Word, our happiness and our victory will never be transient, but will remain for eternity. O Emmy, it's so true: if everything is right between us and God, we'll always be completely happy.

I've just written the enclosed letter to Lucia Franke, clarifying my position yet again. The Lord laid this obligation on me, but simultaneously gave me a peace that is much, much greater than before, and made me even happier about you, my incomparably glorious bride, than I was before. "Then sings my soul, my Savior God to thee: How great thou art! How great thou art!"

Please ask Else to go to Lucia tomorrow or the day after. Have her take a greeting from you as well, with the message that you would also gladly have gone to see her yourself.

Tell Frau Pastor Hachtmann that you are engaged – it's a matter of fact – but don't mention my name, and don't tell her anything else. I don't want her to know more than that.

I can't get Galatians 3:25–27 out of my mind: "Now that faith has come, we are no longer under the supervision of the law. You are all sons of God through faith in Christ Jesus, for all of you who were baptized into Christ have clothed yourselves with Christ." I feel I'm facing tremendous decisions, and I will simply and definitely obey God as soon as I have certainty. But I don't know where I'm going at the moment and am totally confused. Still, I trust Jesus. Follow the Lamb wherever he goes! I'm very happy for that firm direction.

Now I must close, since I have several important letters to write. My dearest, I'm so glad to be able to write to you that I'm once again full of peace and joy. O Emmy, you are more and more glorious to me.

My love for you is becoming so inconceivably great that I'll be surprised if my earthly body endures its overflowing. But Jesus will give me strength to remain peaceful in this joy too. May he bless you, my heart, and be close to you with his mighty spirit and deep love. For he is wonderful, and our counselor, strength, eternal father, and prince of peace.

Be happy, then, my darling and delightful bride. I love you inexpressibly, inconceivably, unconquerably, unbelievably, and unendingly.

Your tempestuous bridegroom

I can't find any good roses for delivery in Brumby. What a shame!

Breslau
September 4, 1907

2 Peter 3:14–15: "So then, dear friends, since you are looking forward to this, make every effort to be found spotless, blameless and at peace with him. Bear in mind that our Lord's patience means salvation, just as our dear brother Paul also wrote you with the wisdom that God gave him."

My glorious bride,

To begin with, I ask your forgiveness for my inner and outer restlessness, which must have been rather obvious to you, since one of my last letters had the wrong postage on it, two addresses were blotted out, a letter I said was enclosed wasn't, and other things like that.

It's been very hard for me to attain real composure. I keep vacillating between restlessness and peace, between fierce pain and sadness, and complete joy – over and over again. I haven't even thanked you for your two sweet letters. Both refreshed me greatly and gave me deep joy. I'm so thankful to God that *you're* truly peaceful in him. Nothing else could strengthen me more than simply knowing this.

Today I prayed a long, long time, and this hour of dedication has brought me to a momentous decision, one which will give our life a clearly defined direction, laden with suffering. You, my beloved, darling Emmy – my brave, faithful bride – are of course the first person I'm telling that, as of today, I have been convinced by God, with quiet and sober biblical certainty, that baptism of believers alone is justified.

Taking Galatians 3:26–27 as a starting point, I persisted in reflecting on Jesus with simple, honest prayer, and have come to feel that scripture recognizes only one baptism: that of those who have become believers. And since scripture is, to me, the revelation of God and his will, fully adequate in itself and incapable of being added to, it reveals to me the will of my God and unmasks the baptism of unbelieving (or more accurately, not-believing) infants as not emanating from the Holy Spirit.

I therefore regard myself as unbaptized and hereby declare war on the existing church system. I'll use until Sunday to educate myself, at least to some extent, as to the state of scholarship on this question and to wait for your opinion. I will then inform our parents on both sides. It is my wish, of course, to be baptized as soon as possible and to leave the established church. You'll help me, however, by remaining completely calm and doing *nothing* hasty.

The position you take on this question, my one and only life companion, will of course have tremendous significance for me. You were in fact already more clear than I. But I implore you to let my decision be only an instigation for you: test this question still more carefully and thoroughly than you did before, but let scripture alone decide the outcome.

I'll be more than happy to wait for you as long as my conscience allows. Should you, contrary to all expectation, be convinced that "infant baptism" is willed by God, I hardly need say that our fellowship will *not* be affected in any way, much as I should like for us to have the same views on this point too.

Let's not say *anything* to *anybody* to begin with. You must on no account even hint at it, until I myself have come out with it. I'll still wait a short time so as to look at all sides of the matter clearly and to allow you time.

What will happen then, the Lord only knows, and that's sufficient. I'll inquire just before the winter semester whether I can still take my exams, and in case the answer is no, I'll immediately switch over to philosophy so that I can still get my Ph.D. as soon as possible. If God wishes and blesses it, maybe we can get married sooner than otherwise. But of course I'm not thinking of that in making this great decision. I am only searching my Christ-bound conscience. I know one thing for sure: that Matthew 19:29 is gloriously true and that Jesus will lead us perfectly. "And everyone who has left houses or brothers or sisters or father or mother or children or fields for my sake will receive a hundred times as much and will inherit eternal life."

I wish you, little darling, the same holy peace I've been granted through Jesus, so that no worry about the future may oppress you, since he cares for you. Trust joyfully in him. The victory is yours.

I can't say how thankful and happy I am that Jesus has given you to me, my dear, dear, dear Emmy! It will be so easy for me to be given up on and misunderstood by everyone, now that I have *you.* But let us pray that our loved ones may be brought closer to Jesus (not the Enemy!) through all this. Because I know it will cause them great pain.

Let's write to each other daily in these important days. Tell me everything you're thinking about and feeling, as completely as you can. I now have regained strength from the Lord. Please write very soon and very warmly to Lucia! It's important, for

Jesus' sake. Write also to Hannah very soon. She'll be coming home in the next few days.

Everyone here greets you. So feel most heartily embraced and take the deepest and warmest kiss from your Ebbo, who loves you beyond all bounds and conceiving.

The wonderful quotation you sent about the sheep of Christ gives me great joy and strengthens me. My deepest thanks!

Breslau
September 6, 1907

1 John 5:3–4: "This is love for God: to obey his commands. And his commands are not burdensome, for everyone born of God overcomes the world. This is the victory that has overcome the world, even our faith."

My glorious bride,

We'll soon have been engaged for half a year. We've already experienced untold happiness, so let's not complain, darling Emmy, if the second half-year opens with what may be difficult family struggles. I think the Lord will grant us marriage sooner than we'd hoped. I have asked him for this in faith because being apart is so hard, and I'm convinced that it is in keeping with God's will that we start a home together as soon as possible. If God helps me with my final exams, as I expect he will, I'll be able to take up von Gerdtell's request to work with him already next fall.

Then, if all goes well, we'll be able to marry around Christmas 1908; that is, in a year and a quarter. Wouldn't that be an overwhelming grace? We'd have been engaged for less than two years!

With regard to baptism, my conviction is so clear to me after the soberest reflection that I now consider a change of mind practically out of the question. I feel as though scales have fallen from my eyes. I haven't found a single verse that proves the efficacy of infant baptism, but I do see quite a number of distinct passages presupposing actual conversion to Christ before baptism. Accordingly, I feel that no baptism exists except that which is based

1) on full acceptance of Christ. Galatians 3:26–27: "You are all sons of God through faith in Christ Jesus, for all of you who were baptized into Christ have clothed yourselves with Christ."

2) on cleansing one's conscience before God. 1 Peter 3:21: "and this water symbolizes baptism that now saves you also – not the removal of dirt from the body but the pledge of a good conscience toward God."

3) and therefore on dying with Christ. Colossians 2:11–12: "In him you were also circumcised, in the putting off of the sinful nature, not with a circumcision done by the hands of men but with the circumcision done by Christ, having been buried with him in baptism and raised with him through your faith in the power of God, who raised him from the dead." Romans 6:2–4: "By no means! We died to sin; how can we live in it any longer? Or don't you know that all of us who were baptized into Christ Jesus were baptized into his death? We

were therefore buried with him through baptism into death in order that, just as Christ was raised from the dead through the glory of the Father, we, too, may live a new life."

The passages about circumcision that I formerly interpreted differently I now understand to mean thus: that in the Old Covenant, Abraham's natural descendants received circumcision soon after birth as his blessing and as the seal of his faith. In the New Covenant, however, only those who follow Abraham as a matter of personal faith are his "children." Romans 4:12: "And he is also the father of the circumcised who not only are circumcised but who also walk in the footsteps of the faith that our father Abraham had before he was circumcised"; and 16–17: "Therefore, the promise comes by faith, so that it may be by grace and may be guaranteed to all Abraham's offspring – not only to those who are of the law but also to those who are of the faith of Abraham. He is the father of us all. As it is written: 'I have made you a father of many nations.' He is our father in the sight of God, in whom he believed – the God who gives life to the dead and calls things that are not as though they were." In accordance with this, only those who have become believers can receive the circumcision of the New Covenant – that is, baptism with water; and they are to do this as young children in Christ – that is, immediately after their conversion.

Nor does Matthew 28:18–20 disprove baptism of believers: "Then Jesus came to them and said, 'All authority in heaven and on earth has been given to me. Therefore go and make disciples of all nations, baptizing them in the name of the Father and of the Son and of the Holy Spirit, and teaching them to obey everything I have commanded you.'" An explanation of the Greek would be too lengthy to include here, but in my opinion the passage should be understood and translated as follows: Make disciples of ("bring to faith") all nations, and in doing so, baptize them and teach them to hold to all they have learned! Nothing is said about the order of events, only that baptizing and teaching go together with bringing people to faith and helping them to subordinate themselves to it. It's part of the same thing – a self-evident supplement.

So in my opinion, the passage doesn't prove anything. At very most, it shows that baptism belongs to becoming a disciple and cannot be separated from that.

I'm still thinking a great deal about all this, but that's enough for now. I only wanted to give you a glimpse into my thoughts. What's decisive for me is not the books I'm reading now, by theologians from within the church and outside it, but the words written by the Spirit in the Bible.

And I want to ask you, my one and only dear, to test the matter with thorough consideration and calm, and not take a definite stand on it until God's will is really clear to you.

I've still got an important question for you. I want to have more clarity in regard to everything before saying anything to my parents, not only about baptism, but about our common future. May I confide in von Gerdtell and ask his advice as to whether I should continue the study of theology? I think he'd know. Or should I wait until my parents know of my new conviction about baptism? What do you think?

It would be a great help to me if I could write to von Gerdtell on Sunday, so as not to lose a single week for my studies, whether I end up in theology or in philosophy. But I don't want to do anything without your agreement beforehand.

Your bridegroom

It wasn't easy living with the Hachtmanns. Emmy enjoyed working with the children, but their mother was critical and demanding, and the pastor had little use for her enthusiastic faith. Emmy's letters from the first part of her stay in Brumby no longer exist, but if Eberhard's repeated words of encouragement are any indication, she was often unhappy there.

Breslau
September 10, 1907

Psalm 34:5: "Those who look upon him are radiant of countenance – they beam with joy – and their faces never grow pale."

My darling little bird,

It gave me great joy to look up and translate the verse above for you. The first phrase is there twice. "Radiant of countenance" stems from the Kautzsch Bible; "beam with joy" (a better translation, in my opinion) comes from a dictionary.

Dear, sweet Emmy: I want to inscribe this deeply on your heart, so that it will always shine out from there: *"They who look upon him beam with joy."* Notice, too, that this verse is from our engagement Psalm! We will praise the Lord *at all times;* his praise shall *evermore* be upon our lips. You see, my sweet bride, it concerns me how quiet and serious you've become in Brumby. Emmy, don't look at the fact that I'm not with you in person or that you have no friends. Don't think about what might follow if we are baptized, or about the Hachtmanns' constant comments and criticisms. Instead, *look upon the Lord* and you will beam with joy!

You'll understand that I don't mean anything unnatural or put on. I just mean that there is freedom from being caught up by dreary thoughts through looking to Jesus. Certainly one cannot ignore how one feels, nor circumstances or conditions as they are. But by looking to Jesus in trust, we can nevertheless always be liberated from all that oppresses and drags us down. Lift your eyes, then, to the sunny heights, up into the heavenly places where Jesus is and where the prayers of your Ebbo are too. *Up to Jesus,* and the joy of victory will be yours! Know that I say all this just as much to myself.

It's good that you're able to distinguish false piety from true Christianity. Anyone who hasn't grasped life according to the word of God isn't reborn and is lost despite the most pious religiosity. This is shown in 1 John 2:3–5: "We know that we have come to know him if we obey his commands. The man who says, 'I know him,' but does not do what he commands is a liar, and the truth is not in him. But if anyone obeys his word, God's love is truly made complete in him"; 2 John 9: "Anyone who runs ahead and does not continue in the teaching of Christ does not have God; whoever continues in the teaching has both the Father and the Son"; the Gospel of John 8:47: "He who belongs to God hears what God says. The reason you do not hear is that you do not belong to God," and many other passages, though these are probably the clearest.

I'm also very happy that you're testing the question of baptism so quietly and unhurriedly. It doesn't surprise me at all that you're taking your time. Neither of us should say anything to anybody until next Sunday, then. We can wait even longer for further clarification if the Lord wishes it, though I'm not in favor of this at the moment. What you write about thinking it over without being influenced is very important. Quite apart from the opinions of people for and against it, we must search scripture, our only authority, and not tolerate any supplementation, not even the smallest addition or subtraction. Jesus warned the Pharisees so sharply against appending and adding to, or watering down and spiritualizing, his words. He also rebuked Herod for trying to go halfway: partly obedient and partly disobedient.

If it's at all possible, we ought to be baptized together. True, I don't really know yet how we'll make it happen, but the Lord will show us. You could, for example, invite yourself to the von Gerdtells, and I could stay with the Maschers. He would be glad to baptize us. Would you like to borrow two books about the questions of baptism and church? I can send them to you.

I'm so glad you wrote that the Lord is always close to you. Yes, he, our glorious king, protects and illumines you.

Loving you eternally and endlessly in him,
your faithful Ebbo

On Sunday I was at the Fellowship for the Lord's Supper, which was held after a clear sermon by our Pastor, Hänisch.

Breslau
September 13, 1907

1 Corinthians 4:20: "For the kingdom of God is not a matter of talk but of power."

My one and only beloved Emmy,

Today, in all quietness, I want to write you more fully. Through the thorough and deep-going time I spent with my dear friend von Gerdtell, I'm filled today in a very special way with the feeling that you, my Emmy, will remain forever the only human being with whom I have complete understanding and am completely at one. Such a firm friendship as that between von Gerdtell and me, united in so many respects and based on Jesus, occurs very seldom, I believe, and on the matter of baptism, too, we understood each other excellently, apart from small details. But that's just why I miss you so terribly and why no friend can replace what you are to me, even in the remotest way. But we can't complain, not even if pain of separation cuts deeply, as now. No, the kingdom of God stands not in words, not in feelings, not in thoughts, but *in strength.*

So I've given my sufferings and longings over to Jesus, and I know that in him I have *the power* to master them. And I've given him even more: namely, all my pushing for union with you as soon as possible.

I've also asked for and received strength from him to help you in this instead of standing in your way and burdening you, as I've done so often – strength to restrain my stormy, passionate nature, which so often has grieved Jesus, and also you, my dearest dear. I thank you for having borne it so patiently. With his strength I *will* be more tender and considerate. I have to learn to control myself better. And I also want to become more like you.

I was just about to thank you for your letter of September 10, and here comes one from the 12th. The whole letter refreshes and gladdens me. I'm especially glad to hear about the beautiful summer weather you're having and to think how you're enjoying it, especially in the garden. I love remembering that wonderful afternoon when we strolled the narrow path through the fields in splendid sunshine, like today's, and were so infinitely happy in Jesus; how we told him this in prayer under the tree and then had coffee together – such a wonderful, undisturbed time, with the peaceful orchard and quiet village in front of us and the pastoral scene behind us. And how we then went back along the lovely path, picking thistles for little Gustav as we went, and talking together about our love and wishing our loved ones the same happiness; how I led you down the steep slope of Greiffenstein, taking care that you wouldn't fall; and how we finally parted on the lawn down below, under the trees, and the glorious hour was over. But one thing is never over, and that is that we will go hand in hand through life and eternity, and that for us there will always be sunshine, because Jesus is our sun. Yes, let's be confident and joyous and praise him for the rest of our lives!

The difficult thing won't be that *we're* forsaken and threatened, but that we'll be the cause of terrible pain to people who are very dear to us, people who deserve more thanks from us

Emmy and Eberhard in Grunewald, 1908

than anyone else. This ought to spur us to a much deeper love for all who are against us. We'll also have to hold firmly to the way of complete obedience in faith. This is the best thing we can give those who are dear to us, though it might not seem like that on the surface. Truth always has a saving and healing effect on the upright. All the more we should pray for our loved ones and be more loving than ever.

Von Gerdtell was extremely loving and so sensible yesterday. He admonished me very earnestly never to place baptism in the foreground, but simply to proclaim Christ, and to see baptism as a natural outcome of that proclamation. I saw this as important already before he said it. We then became clear on the following points, all of which I'll continue to think over until Monday:

1) On Tuesday I'll briefly inform our parents of my conviction, according to which I must (a) be baptized as a believer, since infant baptism is in opposition to what is meant biblically and is therefore not baptism; (b) withdraw from the established church, since I consider it dishonest through and through and contrary to the spirit of the Bible; (c) embrace as my ideal church communities of believing, baptized Christians who use church discipline and celebrate the Lord's Supper.

2) I shall yield to my parents on the matter of timing to the extent that they're honestly willing to give me their reasons against my position and give me the opportunity to respond, my only criterion being scripture, by which I will gladly allow myself to be refuted. I'll then write immediately to Mascher in Steglitz and will presumably be able to be baptized at the end of September or the beginning of October.

3) I'll personally request the General Superintendent (a dreadful title) or Bishop to permit me to take the first exam in spite of my withdrawal from the established church. That's actually not possible, and he won't allow me to do this, but then I'll have done my duty and can switch over to philosophy with a clear conscience. Thus the matter will be completely in God's hands.

4) I can't postpone leaving the established church any more than I can postpone the actual baptism, since I regard the church's deceitful system as Satan's most dangerous weapon and the most treacherous foe of apostolic Christianity. Of course, I don't fail to recognize the uprightness of many churchmen and the fact that they are serious Christians (used by the system to disguise its shamefulness).

5) I will try to get to know the German Baptist churches better, since they have biblical principles, and I will perhaps (though probably not) join them later, since their confession, and to a lesser extent their life, is so in keeping with my ideal.

6) I will be employed by von Gerdtell immediately after my first theology or philosophy exam.

I'd be happy to avoid withdrawing from the church, and will still think it over more carefully in the next days, but whenever I ask my conscience and the Bible, my recognition leaves me no other course. You, of course, need not do this, my little bird, since you're not convinced. I will not send you the book about the history of the struggle between the established church and true church community until I can do without it, perhaps on Monday. You will however receive the one about community and baptism today. Surely my markings, etc., won't bother you.

I was out for a walk with von Gerdtell yesterday, and we prayed and talked over these questions by the banks of a peaceful stream. He also remembered you very well, though I told him very little or hardly anything about us two. You know how reluctant I am to do this because nobody understands it. He said we should move to Marburg later so that we can all become more intimate friends. He had supper with me at home and greeted Papa in a very friendly and polite way.

I am upset that you've already told our secret to Else and that, through her, Frau Baehr also knows! It's so hard to maintain complete silence. But I'm worried now that the story will get around before Monday, because that kind of news moves like lightning. I *hope* Frau Baehr knows that she has to remain completely quiet about it. Have you written to her about this again? My dearest darling, I believe you must learn to guard your tongue. But I've seen how difficult it often is. Von Gerdtell had hardly read the first sentence about my decision to be baptized when he yelled across the corridor to his wife, "Ebbo wants to be baptized." The whole house was rejoicing before he had even read to the end, and I had to pledge him to secrecy.

With regard to the Hachtmanns, I would speak with Frau Pastor on Monday, perhaps by discussing the sacraments with her and letting her know that in your opinion baptism and the Lord's Supper are for believers only. You could say that because of this you're also convinced that you must have yourself baptized. Just don't say it in the form of a solemn statement.

Actually, the difficulty will only come when you *are* baptized. You're under no obligation to give them an account of your opinions, but you'll find out right away what position they take. And that will be very important to know, since we might have to look around for another place for you.

Let's not worry about being baptized together, but leave it to God's leading. Let's just try to be baptized as soon as possible, as soon as our obligations of conscience toward the others are fulfilled.

Your text, "Through faith, Abraham became obedient," gives me much joy and strength. He let himself be led completely by God even though he had no way of knowing how things would turn out. In this way he was blessed and became a blessing for many.

Yes, Frau Baehr is right. It ought to be pure joy that we are considered worthy of suffering for him, our king.

Please write a friendly letter to my parents about baptism – it could be significant as a witness – and reassure them. Of course, this isn't so much your obligation as mine.

Von Gerdtell asked me to take on his printed report this year, and I'll probably have to do it even though I feel the need to study. But until this whole state of affairs gets clear, it won't really be possible. But I'm going to try to do it, and we'll just have to limit our letters to the important things that have to be shared and can't be put off. Next week, of course, will be full of things we'll need to tell each other. Then we'll presumably have to write every day.

Are you reading 1 Corinthians? How far are you? I've wanted to ask.

Now Jesus protect you!
His power is strong.
His peace is deep,
and his blood invincible.

Joshua 1:9: "Have I not commanded you? Be strong and courageous." The prayers of your Ebbo surround you like a wall. And yours are like sunshine to him.

Loving you with the perfect, inexhaustible, eternal love that exists in Jesus alone,

your loyal, faithful Ebbo

Breslau
September 18, 1907

My little bird,

It's only fifteen minutes until 11:30. I hope I can still get this letter into the mail on my bicycle. This morning your Papa's letter arrived, lovingly assuring me that our personal relationship remains as before, as a matter of course. On the other hand he said:

1) that I *must* take the first exam in theology.
2) that we have to limit our letters to twice a week.
3) that I should ask you to hold off with baptism for a year.
4) that we may not see each other for a whole year.

Let us be courageous and trust Jesus. Just before coffee, Hannah came to me very sweetly and wanted to know what was going on – she said I was acting so strangely – and when she asked if I'd received bad news from Halle, I wept like a child, although up to then I'd steadily controlled myself. Then Mama came, worried that one of you had died. So I had to tell her about baptism, whereupon she was extremely loving and tender and said I took everything too seriously and would ruin myself with such excitement. She told me I looked pale and wanted to write to you and tell you to reassure me, otherwise I'd become ill. (That's nonsense, of course.) Then she took me into town with her, bought me chocolate, encouraged me, and was terribly nice. I had little energy, however. One year without you! It weighs on me like a nightmare. It's as if I'm not here.

Yet Emmy, my dearest little bird, Jesus will conquer all the same! To him be praise for everything! I'm sober, but comforted through him. His peace is in me and carries me. After I wrote this, the bicycle lamp went out, and Mama wouldn't let me ride to the station to mail it. I hope you're not waiting for it. This morning I received yours, so sweet and blessed, and Papa's letter, which is on the whole very loving.

It's a terrific joy to me, my darling, that the Lord gave you the firmness to take an attitude to Papa's letter. Yes, *God* must lead us, not people. He will also decide about our seeing each other again and will bring it about excellently. He will now take us at our word and see whether we can joyfully bear everything for him. And we ought to thank him for giving us his strength.

Papa is right about the theology exam. It's simply an obligation I have. We can't make any promises as far as seeing each other and writing, however. But other than that, we'll obey our parents as long as we possibly can. I therefore ask you to find strength in the Lord so that we write to each other only twice a week *as a rule.* We'd planned to do that in any case, a long time ago, isn't that so? Until Sunday we'll still write to each other daily, though. Afterward you can decide what to do.

As for Papa's letter to me, I'm forwarding it to you only reluctantly. Realize that men always write to each other as objectively as possible and leave their feelings out of it. You'll see that the end of the letter is still very kind and loving.

If only I could speak to my father soon! But he's perpetually unavailable. Of course, I must not precipitate anything. The way Jesus leads is the best way.

And now, my Emmy, let's gather strength in prayer and in the Word, strength to look toward him and to trust him in utter simplicity! May he lead us in such a way that we do nothing wrong and always remain in his peace. His word will remain our only authority. Let us hold to nothing but Jesus as he is revealed to us. May he be praised from our whole hearts and make us happy and victorious!

Loving you in him more deeply, firmly, faithfully, and strongly than ever before, I belong to you forever,

your Eberhard

Mama has continued to be extremely loving to me, and so have my brother and sisters. The fellowship I have with Hannah in word and prayer refreshes me too. I pray constantly for you. Jesus hears us. Kissing you 1000 times, your old Ebbo. Papa will probably become a synod/church council member. By faithfulness and love we'll overcome the whole family's attitude soon. May Jesus save them all!

Separation

As the desire to obey and submit to their parents vied with demands of conscience, intense conflicts developed in both Eberhard and Emmy's families. It was hard to see the way forward: As a matter of honor, Eberhard felt he could not renege on the agreement he had made with Heinrich von Hollander to earn his doctorate before marrying. The step of believer's baptism, however, would make him ineligible to sit for his doctoral exam in theology, and in the end, a switch from theology to philosophy became necessary. Out of respect to Emmy's parents, the couple did reduce their rate of correspondence, although they more than made up for it by turning their letters into lengthy epistles with almost daily entries.

In Emmy's next letter, "Gretchen" is her sister, who died of appendicitis in 1903 at age fourteen. Emmy was caring for Gretchen when she died and the experience turned her irrevocably toward Jesus.

Brumby
October 12, 1907

My dearest Ebbo,

Your dear, sweet letter, your poems, and the rose and violets brought me tremendous joy. I had been so sad today, the anniversary of Gretchen's death. It was all so vivid before my eyes, and Monika, who was here for some days, left at eleven o'clock. Frau Hachtmann gave her a big bunch of dahlias from the garden to take along, but she cried her heart out and wanted to stay with me. My dear, dear Ebbo, if only you were here and I could tell you everything.

I still think Gretchen must have seen Jesus at the hour of her death. How else could it have been that she was transfigured; that she looked forward to heaven with so much joy and said, moving her arms as if she were trying to fly, "Oh, that's beautiful, so beautiful!" And after she died, she lay in her little bed with such a peaceful face. It was about five in the morning when Papa, Olga, Heinz, and Monika came (Else was in bed with appendicitis too), and the nurses' choir sang, "Mid the lilies blooming yonder you shall wander; soar, O soul, to heaven fly!"

When it was light, we went home to dress for mourning, and then I went to the Deaconesses' Home to prepare Gretchen's body. How lovely she was as she lay there in her white robe with a myrtle garland on her head, a wreath of violets on her breast, beautiful white lilies around her head, an enormous palm leaf at her feet, and in her folded hands a bouquet of roses. She was with the Lord. How glorious it will be when we can meet her there and praise Jesus in eternity! But God is merciful in allowing us to live so that we may win people for him, and in leading us together so wonderfully so that we can serve him and help each other to give up everything that doesn't please him. There's still an endless amount of that in me. But, thanks to God, he has borne the guilt, and he cleanses us; therefore our lives belong to him!

Your poems are sweet, my Ebbo. I've sent you some of mine. You know, since Gretchen's death I really haven't written any poems, since I realize that I don't have that talent. Nor do I have any time for it here. If I should write one some day, I'll send it to you. You're right, I do have much more substance now through Jesus and through you.

There's some mission event at the church today at two o'clock, and unfortunately I have to go with the children. I'd much rather write to you, since I don't think it will be important. We're having really hot summer weather, and I'm wearing one of my thin blouses. I hope it'll stay like this for a long time. I don't like winter at all!

You know, I'm so happy that I can tell you about myself and that I don't need to gloss over my sins, but can simply tell you how everything is, and that we can bring it all together before the Lord. As he said, "If two of you are united in asking for something, I will do it for you." Ebbo, we can never give thanks enough for that!

Today I have something on my heart and want to ask your advice. You see, I want to do *everything* for Jesus, but there are many things I do that I'm unsure of, and because of this I can't be truly happy doing them. For example, when there's bowling on Sunday afternoon, or when I'm asked to play some overture as a piano duet with Herr Pastor, or when I'm supposed to read some book – I can't say, "I'm doing this in the name of Jesus." It wouldn't be genuine. What do you think about this? I've worried that if I did it joyfully and willingly, I might forget that I am doing it for Jesus and would then be doing it for my own pleasure. Do you understand?

Then today I told a lie. I was terribly frightened when I realized it. We were sitting together in the evening, and I went upstairs for half an hour or so to write to you. When I came down, Frau Pastor asked me where I'd been, and I made up something that I hadn't been doing at all. How can that happen, that I tell a lie without even a thought? I've begun to wonder whether I'm completely dishonest, since this kind of thing happens to me so often. I'm terribly depressed about it. You'll surely be sad, too, but I must tell you about it anyway. It would be terrible if you discovered something like that about me only later. If only the Lord would completely free me from this sin!

Kissing you with great love,
your faithful bride

Unsure of how to resolve the growing rift between them and their families, the separated couple made independent visits to the von Hollander parents to explain their position and plead for leniency. But it was to no avail, and difficult scenes ensued.

Breslau
October 27, 1907

Trust in Jesus alone.

My dear, sweet Emmy,

We're now at a juncture at which we must witness to Jesus as our Lord and complete victor in a particular way.

My little bird, I know it's an extremely difficult time for both of us. We don't know when we'll see each other next, though this is our greatest and deepest heart's desire. It's also our natural right and a divine gift that belongs to us.

I think I may have acted clumsily yesterday. I spoke the truth rather forcefully, especially to your Mama and Olga, though I believe I said too little rather than too much. The situation demands, above all, truth and clarity. I don't regard my conversation with your Papa as finished either. I told him that I can't accept his attitude, since the assumptions that underlie his actions are false. I've not forgotten his statement that under the present circumstances he would never have permitted our engagement until I had found employment. He said this very decidedly. That's very nice, but we *are* already engaged, more so than two people ever – or hardly ever – have been. Papa is simply trying to reduce our contact to a minimum in whatever way he can. I find it unjust, cruel, and irresponsible and told Mama and Olga this in an energetic fashion, which made a deep impression on them. I don't regret one word.

In fact, it seems Papa is softening, because he repeatedly explains to me that he isn't a stickler for principles but has acted completely according to the present situation. This implies that any change in the situation could bring him to remove his prohibition if he sees fit. But we mustn't overestimate him. Above all, let us praise God that we *are engaged* and that the glorious times we have behind us will yield the most precious memories. After such experiences of our love and God's grace, we should be thankful to God that he allows us to correspond as engaged people who know each other fully and know ourselves to be united. It could so easily be otherwise. But how should we conduct ourselves now, practically speaking? I'll write to Papa once more, plainly, decisively, and with love. He was, by the way, very nice to me during our talk, embracing me and squeezing my hand again and again, etc. At one point I think he was also deeply touched. The others were all weeping more or less. I kept a tight rein on myself. It's such a joy that Else is coming to be with you. O Emmy!

My love: like me, you must above all become inwardly free of *all* resentment and *all* bitterness. Jesus has given me full victory in this regard, and I can't thank him enough for it. As concerns our contact, we must resolutely make arrangements with a view to a long separation. Let's write and tell each other everything, even more conscientiously than before. Like you, I will write every day from now on and send off the letter twice a week as we have been doing. You, my darling, must be sure to take a quiet hour at midday, now more than ever. This must not be denied you on any account, or else you'll have to write at night. If you must, of course, you'll still do it.

Our contact by letters during this next year will be of great significance for our future. Above all, my dear little bird, *always* write to me when you're downcast or need to cry, when you feel miserable or have no strength or joy. I place the greatest value on this. I must know *exactly* how you're feeling. I'll do just the same naturally. God forbid that you should have to lapse into poor health to convince your parents of their injustice. That would be just too dreadful. The thought of it gives me a cold shiver. Yesterday I felt at times like a severely ill or dying man – that's how deeply the thought of your suffering for Jesus' sake gripped me.

My Emmy, two things are needed now above all else: *silence* and *love!*

1) Silence! Jesus is in us, and we in him. *He* has permitted everything to happen, to our best interests. Without his will, not a hair of your head will be lost. Thus we can and must trust him. He *will* lead us. Everywhere, on every path, his blessing is with us. Perhaps we won't see each other for a whole year – he will even bless that separation, if only we humble ourselves and believe in him. And he will test us, too, to make sure we're not idols for one another, but that we love and trust God above everything. Let us therefore look up to him and not grow pale. May the Lord rather give us the strength and grace to demonstrate what Christians are able to endure.

2) Love! We must nurture only the best, holiest, deepest feelings to our parents and Olga. They are in error and are

only making themselves unhappy. More than ever, we should express our love and respect to them. (Papa has already said that he esteems my character all the more highly because of my conduct and convictions regarding baptism.)

Now, to close: I pray for you more earnestly and deeply than ever, my love! May he give you victory with your parents, with the Hachtmanns, and with the children in your care – and victory most of all in your own heart, so that you can have peace and joy just as surely as you have the love of your Ebbo.

Persevering always and forever in prayer, strengthened by all opposition, and completely and fully in Jesus,

I remain *yours*

Halle
October 29, 1907

My dearest Ebbo,

Ebbo, I believe our witness is really having an effect. Mama cries all the time, and today she said she believed Papa would retract his demands, because it just couldn't go on like this. This morning I was singing from the *Blankenburg Songbook,* and Mama cried throughout. She badly wants to revoke Papa's rules. I have faith that God will soon give us a meeting.

In deepest love,
forever your faithful Emmy

Conflicts developing within the Student Christian Movement added to Eberhard's difficulties. One involved a comment made by one of his colleagues in the leadership questioning the authorship of the Second Letter of Peter and its validity. Von Gerdtell, Eberhard, and others protested, asserting that scripture must be accepted unconditionally as God's word. With no compromise in sight, a split seemed likely.

Breslau
October 29, 1907

"Peace in the Lord! When grief oppresses you, Jesus, who strengthens every heart, is near."

My sweetest Emmy,

I can hardly imagine a situation in which I could long for you more deeply, more invincibly, and more urgently – to be comforted by your eyes, your hands, your words, your prayers, your presence! It almost seems as if the Lord permitted this so as to test me, to see whether I can carry a heavy burden for him even without your help. It seems the Lord wants to ask me, "Can you follow me with a full and joyful heart even when separated from *her?*" O Emmy, I haven't been able to answer this question yet with a wholehearted yes. Yes, I can follow with my *whole* heart. But a joyful one? I don't know.

Certainly it's a matter of "only" (!) one year, but so far each day is one of unending torture. My only comfort is 1) *Jesus!*

After all, I know that what *he* allows to happen to me must be good, no matter how it looks. 2) *You!* The knowledge that my best beloved is praying especially for me right now and thinking of me is a deep comfort. And so, in spite of my deep sadness, I can say, *I have peace in Jesus and in you!*

The fact that you, sweet darling, write that your father's prohibition might be revoked at Christmas is very loving of you and shows your parents' inner uncertainty and sympathy. But we must not forget how difficult it would be for Papa to take back an edict that he expressed so definitely. It's practically impossible without conversion. I won't believe it before he promises it to you or me in a clear-cut way.

O Emmy, how shocked I was when I suddenly realized that I sent off my last letters to Halle without showing them to you. Forgive me! That was wrong of me, since I'd promised to always pass important things to your parents by you beforehand. It distresses me that I have again been so unreliable. The letters themselves, of course, I don't regret. I *had* to write them, especially the one to Papa, even if it provokes great dissension, etc.

I believe we must be inwardly prepared not to see each other until my exam in September 1908, though the Lord alone knows the future. What all will happen then is also unsure. In everything we are in his hands alone, since I don't have a single friend on whom I can count, because I live to please *no one but Jesus. He* suffices! In him we can live without worries. The situation with the SCM is tragic. If you really want all those long SCM committee letters, let me know. I'll send them to you as soon as you ask.

Brumby
November 10, 1907

My Ebbo,

This morning around ten I was sitting at the piano with the children, singing Christmas carols, when all of a sudden the bell rang and in came Papa and Mama. What a joy! Papa and I talked a little about you, but he didn't really say much. All the same, it's still possible he'll back down on his demands.

But now I have a very important question for you. I was wondering, recently, if it would be better for us to wait with getting baptized until we're married, since after our wedding we won't be restricted by our parents. I don't know, but I find it hard to imagine that I'll have joy in being baptized if it involves going totally against the will of the parents given to me by God. Then, too, since God has destined us for one another forever, it would seem right that we should have ourselves baptized *together,* and as things stand now, that definitely won't work. Of course, if you feel that postponing baptism means allowing ourselves to be hindered in our conversion to Jesus, then I think we should do it immediately! What do you think? Please write about this as soon as possible. I should add that if we are going to wait for a year, then we might as well wait even a bit longer. God would see that we are still observing his commandments.

By the way, when I was at home two weeks ago, Stenzel asked me about baptism, and I told him that I was for it, despite the wishes of my parents. He thought that I should wait until our wedding, as a sign of obedience. If our parents were trying to mislead us to some sin, he said, that would be different.

I don't know if I'm expressing myself clearly enough. Nor am I at all certain that the Lord wants it like this, which is all that matters. Of course I haven't said anything about this to anyone, but the thought did come to me whether our anxieties, etc., weren't for nothing, since if we have to wait one year anyway, why not even a little longer? Well, God will show us the right moment at all events. Please pray very earnestly that we don't cave in, on the one hand, but don't become too stubborn, either. I'll do this too.

But now, my darling, good night! May Jesus be with us in everything we do.

Your Emmy

Breslau
November 12, 1907

My bride,

I still have a huge assignment to finish, but I'm enormously pleased how the Lord is helping me in my studies. And I pray for you often and am happy in our great love and in our fellowship with Jesus.

I'm terribly sorry for Betty. We talked today, occasioned by the imminent death of Mimi Cornill, who is consumptive. We discussed the power of life in Christ and the decline of every life that doesn't dwell in him. I'm more and more certain that Betty doesn't possess new life in and for Jesus, although she comforts herself with the forgiveness of her Savior. Obviously I hope that she will still be saved, but that won't be possible without complete surrender.

Yesterday at noon I unfortunately behaved very badly. Mama made hurtful allusions to your Papa's gruffness, teased me about our correspondence, and needled me about my last trip to Halle (she suspects I saw you), and I got so furious that I jumped up, leaving my food on the table, and slammed several doors. I wasn't able to calm down for a long time. Only after a long struggle in prayer did Jesus overcome and calm me down, and I then put things right with everyone.

This is what happened: Betty got upset that you sent the letter she wrote to you back to me, especially because in it she had called me "sunshine." During the ensuing scene, she rightly called me "Mr. Gloomy." It's true I look terribly grim when I'm angry. But I was so happy afterward, when everybody forgave me. I asked them very energetically, however, not to be so tactless in the future, and they promised me they wouldn't. Betty thinks I'm too touchy, and that Mama hadn't really said anything. That's true too. The slightest lack of sensitivity about our relationship enrages me. May Jesus help me in this! Incidentally, I notice again and again how they actually love you terribly much. And they have the deepest respect for your father.

The meeting on Sunday refreshed me deeply, as did the bike ride I took the same night on a lonely road. You know how I love doing that! My acetylene lantern burns really well, like a proper searchlight.

First we had a gathering for the young adults about the end of Hebrews 11 and 12:1–2. I had a little prayer-room to myself before the main evening gathering, which I addressed. I tried to awaken my audience in the strength of the Spirit. Several were in tears, although I spoke in a rather general, pastoral way. After the meeting a few people came up to me, among them a woman who'd been converted in last year's awakening meetings. (I've told you a great deal about the grace of those meetings.) She told me that the Enemy had taken away her strength recently. Another woman felt unable to confess her sins and was very unhappy because of that. The three of us prayed together, and Jesus was close to us. Dear Emmy, this is a small blessing. Actually, every blessing is great, but we must, in humility and brokenness, give honor to *Jesus alone* for even the greatest and most powerful blessing. This holds true for everything: studies, meetings, opportunities for witnessing, struggles with sin, etc. Yes, to him be all the honor!

I've been waiting all day for a letter from you. I'll send off this one anyway. What's wrong with the postal service?

In great love,
your faithful bridegroom

Brumby
November 14, 1907

My Ebbo,

I got your letter earlier today and thank the Lord that something came out of it *for him* on Sunday. Yes, that's what we want to do together in the future: lead others to him.

I'm sad you were so impetuous recently. Ebbo, rather let it out on *me* than on others when you're angry. You know, hard as it might be, I always understand you, and I know how sad you are about yourself afterward. Others don't. Please, *please* pull yourself together in front of others. I'd rather you vented at me instead. Of course I, too, can't stand it when anyone dares to make comments about our relationship, but it's enough that Jesus and we know how wonderful and deep it is.

Yours happily, Emmy

Breslau
November 14, 1907

My sweet, darling Emmy,

I've been reading Spurgeon's *All of Grace* and have been deeply refreshed by it. I want to send it to you tomorrow so you can read it all the way through.

Otherwise I've been miserable. In the first place I was exhausted from studying and by yesterday's SCM bible class, and had heart palpitations and a poor night. And today I don't have any energy and have a mild headache, etc. On top of this I unfortunately got into another argument with Mama, who made unfounded and unprecedented reproaches against me. I got extremely angry and let fly at her. I only shouted but would have relished throwing the lamp on the floor and smashing it.

Jesus was able only gradually to become master over me – he, who *always* bore injustice so calmly! Afterward, of course, I felt terrible about how I acted. But Jesus saves and will also redeem me from my passionate and miserable nature. You have no notion how I despise myself. Oh, let's pray and pray again that we learn to believe in Jesus more! He shall overcome fully And as annoying as she is, Mama is actually very kind and loving. She doesn't hold it against me for even half a day when I've done something like that. I love her terribly.

You know, there's a lot of truth in the saying, "An anxious man is open to the devil." That's another reason we should both pay close attention to our health. Sleep is always very important for me: If I don't get it, things go badly immediately; and when I catch up on it, everything goes better again. I'm no Hercules, of course, but I'm mostly tough and resilient, so don't fret yourself too much. You hear me, darling?

Today's letter from you – No. 145 – is so refreshing. I'm glad you're feeling more cheerful and steady again. Let's always be there for each other, my Emmy. This time it's me again who especially needs help.

I'm going to bed now, so as to be on top of things tomorrow. I trust Jesus, and that's enough. Isaiah 40:26 and 40:31 are a great source of strength for me. Good night. His might and strength are so great that no one can fail.

November 15

As often happens, dinner is so late today that I'm using the time to read your sweet letter and answer it. God greatly blessed me today: I'm strong and cheerful again, and my work went well; and most important, he overcame the strong temptations that came over me last night and this morning. It was so awful that I almost wrote to your father asking if he wouldn't give in and let us see each other. I would a thousand times more prefer having my back lashed into a bloody welt than to have my heart ripped from my body because of being kept from you. I'm in danger of growing bitter – I would have liked to rebuke Papa for his brutality and crudity toward his own children. Why am I writing you all this, since I'm actually sorry for deserting the Lord like I've done? I guess because you yourself know the need for us to show each other our hearts' deepest corners, and I don't want to make any exceptions.

Jesus has given me victory, and his heart has become mine again. My old, bad, proud, passionate heart no longer belongs to me. He has taken it away. Because of this, I trust that in him I will fully conquer all evil thoughts and remain in his love. It's just a terrible temptation when I think about ourselves, not to mention our parents. But I ought to look away, completely away from all that, and look to *him!* Then I can love and bless everyone. Hallelujah!

In the meantime, don't worry about my well-being. I know myself too well not to realize that this little bit of excitement will be forgotten in a short time. The Lord will lead us. We must simply be faithful in everything and not make a battle plan.

In love, your Ebbo

As soon as they had agreed to postpone their baptisms for a year, Emmy's parents gave Eberhard and Emmy permission to spend the Christmas holidays together. Emmy wrote, "I'm sure that my willingness to oblige them was right and willed by God. It wasn't easy, since I'm very stubborn by nature. I intend to keep asking my parents for permission to be baptized as soon as I'm convinced it's what God wants; but I'd never be happy acting against their express prohibition, as long as they don't add other obstacles." Meanwhile, Eberhard struggled to escape the doldrums of endless studies (and endless family quarrels). As he wrote in a long letter on November 17, "This week was very hard. The main reason, I'm afraid, was that several times I forgot about Jesus. Besides, my studies were very difficult...and family matters very sad. The Student Christian Movement crisis, the issue of baptism, the uncertainty of my future – all this drained my courage and strength. So far, however, the Enemy has not been able to get me down, because Jesus has protected me and I keep taking refuge under his cross! He remains my salvation, my sun, my shield. He is my staff in the valley of gloom. And he will and must lead everything gloriously." By December, this faith had indeed changed Eberhard's outlook, and he was once more writing cheerful letters.

Brumby
December 6, 1907

My Ebbo,

I received your lovely, long letter yesterday afternoon and have read it several times. Thank you for describing Hermann and Käthe's wedding in such detail. It must have been very nice. Of course, I also missed Jesus in it all – that has to be the main thing for us. And there won't be dancing at our wedding. Can you imagine the apostles dancing? I can't.

I'm in suspense about where we'll end up this Christmas – at your parents' house or mine? Unfortunately I can't write much this week; we're very busy at the moment and I don't have any time. By the way, the little stars you sent are so sweet, and the little tree.

I visited three sick people this afternoon and brought them something to eat. Of course I said something about Jesus in each place. I find it difficult here, though, since there is very little longing for God and everyone seems to be self-satisfied. O Ebbo, if only I could talk everything over with you! I'm looking forward to this tremendously. I'm also feeling the need to take time to experience God quietly, and not to be in such a rush all the time.

United in him forever by our unique love,
your loyal bride

Breslau
December 17, 1907

My glorious bride,

Since you're celebrating your birthday early, I also want to take part in it, even if we can't be together, so I'm sending you Kühn's book. I'm also enclosing the story of the "Prodigal Sons," for Annemarie. We can get her something else if she has it already. If she doesn't, please inscribe something in it for her.

I'm in the peace of Jesus, though there are still two things that bother me a little at the moment. The first is that I have a toothache *and* a headache for the third time within days. The second is that when I was reading the newspaper today, I suddenly felt such distress and sadness about the state of the world. Oh, how I hate it! The desperate unhappiness of the masses shatters me. We think far too seldom of how millions of people around us are going to ruin, are racing toward hell, while so few – so tragically few – stop and save them in the power of Jesus' spirit! O Emmy, it's terribly hard to sit here and pile up knowledge day after day when I think of everything that's happening outside in the meantime. On the other hand, it's good, because it makes me see how wretched and helpless I am – that I am nothing. But let's pray earnestly all the same that God saves as many as possible through his servants and that he prepares both of us for this service.

My little darling, if only you were here! There's so much to tell each other. I long to pour out my heart to you but haven't been able to for almost four months. I look forward tremendously to finally talking over *everything* with you and learning from you in everything. What happiness it will be to pray with you! What bliss to see your eyes; to look deep into them; to kiss your sweet mouth; to have you, my only love, beloved beyond understanding, so close to me as my bride, my heart, and my better self!

Be sure we have enough time to be together. I'm not going to let you return to Brumby in less than two weeks, you heavenly, golden possession! Just be emphatic and cheerfully make it clear to Frau Pastor that you won't be coming back in any less than three weeks, because you also need to spend time at home. Do you think that will work? How are they going to manage without you, by the way? Can you ask them whether they'll really still need you, once they've made a new arrangement with their maid?

If I get a letter from you tomorrow morning, I'll write more. But for now, good night. O Emmy, I just wrote a very stormy poem about you. I'll enclose it, as it shows my deepest self and the way I often feel. I think you'll have to calm me down a little when you finally come. We'll have to ask the Lord to smooth the turbulent waves of my heart by his peace, so that the words, "Here is the faith and patience of the holy ones!" become truth in me. Let's patiently trust his leading. That is what will make our happiness last forever.

Looking forward beyond words to seeing you,
your loyal Ebbo

Your letter hasn't come yet, but I have to send mine off.

Brumby
December 18, 1907

My most deeply beloved Ebbo,

This is just a short but warm word of thanks for the beautiful book and for your dear letter. You're really too sweet. Your gift for Annemarie and the box also made me very happy.

Today I had another unpleasant incident with Frau Pastor. We were out walking together, and I told her I thought it might be better if I stayed home after Christmas. I said I was sorry to do this, but felt I needed to take time off for reasons of health. She replied that neither she nor her husband were in agreement with this and said I ought to think it over some more.

She said they didn't want to hold me but wanted, nonetheless, to speak with Mama or Papa and present their side. When I said I'd be happy for that – that I'd ask Papa to visit them around Christmas – she said that wouldn't do either and there was no point in it. I'll tell you everything in person before I say anything at home, because Papa will surely start a big commotion again, and for Jesus' sake I'd rather avoid any unnecessary scenes. But I think I won't go back to the Hachtmanns after Christmas. Could you please start thinking about another place for me instead? The situation here is getting impossible, although I'm sure I'm to blame as well. I'll tell you everything when we're together. They were very nice to me in the end, but that just makes it a better time to leave. I've tried it for nearly four months. I told Frau Pastor that I'd never been involved in anything as unpleasant as my experiences in Brumby and that she could ask the Freybes or inquire at the hospital, etc., to verify this.

But enough of that. I'm happy that I have you and will see you so soon and can tell you everything. How I look forward to praying with you! Jesus protect us both until we meet again!

In him always,
your faithful Emmy

By Degrees

Eberhard and Emmy's elation, when her train finally pulled into the Breslau station on December 22, can only be imagined. Eberhard's parents let down their guard and welcomed their prospective daughter-in-law with unexpected warmth. After a happy Christmas spent talking, walking, reading together, and talking more, the young couple took a train to Halle, where they planned to celebrate New Year's Day with Emmy's family.

That reunion was less pleasant, however, and the visit was marked by accusations, squabbles, and tense scenes. Eberhard left for Breslau with the firm intention of working harder than ever at his studies in order to get his degree at the earliest possible date. But even this impetus for academic rigor couldn't dampen his enthusiasm for evangelizing, and he was soon guiding bible discussions among young people in the nearby town of Brockau.

Emmy, meanwhile, decided not to return to the Hachtmanns in Brumby, and remained in Halle. She wasn't idle long. Remembering Eberhard's exhortation to "always stand on a foundation of rock and save others from sinking," she joined the Young Women's Union, an association linked with the YWCA.

Halle
February 17, 1908

My darling Ebbo,

Your letter, the two charming cards, and the marvelous songbook have been a continual joy to me today. You are much too good to me. Of the songs by Kühn, I think "The Church," "Jesus Alone," and "Heal, O Lord, thy people" are especially beautiful, though "Near to Jesus" is actually the best. It's my favorite apart from "In humility and awe." Which is yours?

Tell me, Ebbo: why couldn't you sleep Saturday night? Did you have heart palpitations again? Please take care of yourself, darling.

I'm glad God is helping you focus on your studies. I also want to thank him for his blessing on the meeting in Brockau. Oh, if only *many* people could be converted to Jesus! I just can't understand why so few come to him. After all, no one who does has ever been disappointed. On the contrary, they've found true life and full contentment in him.

Yesterday evening's fellowship meeting was, I think, greatly blessed. Mama came too. The event opened with the song, "Do you have Jesus, do you have peace?" Then a brother spoke about the Paschal Lamb in the Old and New Testaments. He also told a wonderful anecdote about how the Great Elector [Frederick of Saxony] is said to have had a rope pulled through town every year, and any criminal who took hold of this rope was pardoned. Many didn't dare to grasp the rope because they were ashamed to show themselves in front of a crowd, or for other reasons. That's how it is with Jesus: everyone who grasps onto him will be pardoned, yet so few are willing to do so. After this we all sang, and then Pastor Vonhof spoke in a cheerful and decisive manner. We then sang, "There is still room. God's house is not yet full," and ended with a prayer and closing verse: "Come, with your homesick heart, home to God's bosom of peace."

The meeting was followed by another gathering, especially for anyone who wanted to be converted. On the way home, Else and I encouraged a young woman to decide for Jesus, since she'd been touched by the spirit of the meeting. I don't know whether Mama was touched or not, but she doesn't have any excuse, since she heard the message. And she did admit that much of it had been good.

An earlier meeting that I attended in the afternoon, on the topic of fellowship, was not as blessed, at least not for me. There was too much emphasis on "remaining inside the established church," especially by Fassmer. Great regret was also expressed that so many believers are no longer attending the Lord's Supper at church, but rather celebrating it among themselves in private homes. Amazingly, Hobbing was the one who was the most vocal in favor of forming an "alliance." He even prayed "for Christians who think differently but with whom we are united, as long as they have Jesus." Frau Baehr and Sister Riedel were also there, by the way.

You won't believe the kind of slander I heard about the baptizers recently. It's said that they're holding baptisms at night in the Saale River. Isn't that crazy? Even more shocking, some were kicked out of the Union House because of a rumor that Kühn had said something blasphemous in a lecture he gave on the established church. It's impossible: a pastor who denies that Jesus is the son of God is allowed to preach Sunday after Sunday, but anyone who dares to say anything about the established church is thrown out.

Else isn't doing any work directly for Jesus at the moment. She says she just can't participate in the Young Women's Union, although she often goes there and invites unconverted young women to the meetings. She says it isn't joyful and purposeful enough for her to be a co-worker there. Personally, I'm grateful that it's possible for me to work for Jesus there. Olga is the same: good-natured in many ways but very difficult at times. She needs our love. Monika is getting rather worldly again, whereas Heinz is visibly moved. He came to us beaming with happiness after reading in his Bible and realizing how wonderfully God helps those who trust him. Of course, now he's been forbidden to read "so much" in the Bible.

Incidentally, Ebbo, the Hachtmanns will be here for the mission conference from the 23rd until the 26th and want to visit us while they're here. I'll be friendly to them, but also decisive. I'm not going back to Brumby.

Henny Zabeler just came by and asked me to invite you to her wedding on March 3. There'll be hardly anyone there from Halle, so no one will notice that we're on familiar terms. Of course, I'll only go if you also come.

I must close now. May Jesus protect you and bless your work.

Your bride

Breslau
February 19, 1908

Jesus is everything!

My sweetest Emmy,

Thank you for your loving lines on Sunday's card and Monday's letter. I read them both over and over, and they've made me so happy that I simply can't contain my joy. The blessing God has given me in you is a very important one, as we've told each other often, of course. Before I met you, I'd completely forgotten how to come out of myself and give myself as I am. Everything I had learned about human nature made me close in on myself more and more and give out only what I hoped would be of use to others. I never trusted another person fully and completely, and whenever I confided even a few of my deepest thoughts and feelings, I was severely let down. Having experienced this, I came to believe that true friendship is as rare as a diamond among the billions of rocks on the earth. Then someone – you – came into my life who is as pure and clear as crystal, as radiant and beaming as the sun, so precious and delightful that she seems not to be of the earth. And God gave her to me!

You wouldn't believe, Emmy, how much good it does me to be able to write down everything that's on my heart like this. Darling, my love for you is so boundless, so deep and urgent, that there's nothing to compare it to!

Yes, it would be glorious if I could see you on Sunday, but that won't be possible. It will also be impossible for me to come to Henny Zabeler's wedding. I just can't get away without neglecting my duties here as a disciple of Jesus.

First, I can't be interrupted and distracted from my studies. I need to have everything wrapped up before the written exam in the second half of March.

Second, I can't possibly leave here next Sunday on account of the young people in Brockau. It's significant for eternity when even ten people desire to see the seriousness of their sins and to experience the saving power of Jesus.

Aside from all this, my parents would be greatly offended if I traveled off on such a "frivolous" mission as a wedding while the semester's in session. So as nice as it would be, my darling, it really won't work.

The situation here at home is sometimes very difficult for me. Not that they're unfriendly to me, but there's no understanding between us. Mama says I'm almost worse in submitting to her than Hermann is! Well, there are things that I justifiably want, and I don't like being brushed aside like a little child. I've just been praying about this. On the one hand, Jesus wants us to give our coat as well, to go the second mile. On the other hand, we shouldn't be slaves of people, but men in Christ. Perhaps now you'll understand why I'm so eager for the day I'm no longer tied to my parents. It's frustrating to have one's freedom and independence limited, but the Lord gives me the patience I need over and over again.

My favorite songs? Definitely "I look," "Near to Jesus," the sunshine song, and "Jesus, Savior of my soul." But I also like the ones you named.

You asked about my not sleeping well. I don't know whether it's from overwork, but I sometimes lie awake for hours, and that's no fun. I'm going to stop taking midday naps completely; maybe that will help. The heart palpitations weren't all that disturbing.

Yes, Emmy, we must give thanks for Brockau. But such a blessing is very humbling, because I am so unworthy. This evening one of the young people is coming to see me, tomorrow I'm to speak with two others, and ten of them have asked for personal talks on Sunday. Pray that all goes well. Unless *God* wins their hearts, it's futile and any success is an evil illusion.

In my studies of church history I recently found mention of an interesting custom among the German "Dunkers," now settled in America. The candidate kneels down in the water and in so doing actually baptizes himself. I imagine he or she wears a garment similar to the capes of earlier times. By the way, since the distinguishing characteristic of baptism is confession, I've come to feel that everything about it must be appropriate for the public, and that it should take place in a public area.

That was a digression, I know. But I wanted to write down what I've been thinking on the topic, since I'll probably be baptized in October, unless the Lord has something else in mind.

Now to quite another subject: it's unbelievable, but Mama recently complained that I'm using too much sugar for hot chocolate. She claimed I use a pound a day, which is nonsense. When Papa heard us, he took my side, and then said that no matter what I was consuming, it was having a good effect and that he was glad I looked so healthy. Afterward he took me aside and said I should feel free to take as much as I want, and that he'd pay for it if Mama wouldn't. Isn't that hilarious? First Betty and I and then everybody else laughed ourselves silly. As touching as Papa is, I must say I'd feel guilty of unmanliness if I let myself be squeezed into so lamentable a corner while supposedly being the head of the household.

Thank you for everything you told me about your sisters. Do you read together often, and how do you like Else's Elberfeld translation of the Bible? Don't you also think it helps clarify a lot?

So the Hachtmanns are on the horizon. Sound the alarm! Be sure you're prepared beforehand so that you don't allow yourself to be intimidated for even a moment, and don't accept any of their accusations of untruthfulness. Not allowing yourself to be taken to task for sins you never even committed is part of witnessing to Christ. There's a big difference between untruthfulness and being unclear or confused.

Please hold off the Zabelers. I hope they don't intend to write to me. I'm actually glad I can't go to Henny's wedding. I'll send them a telegram, however. I'm going to write to Papa von Hollander about Sunday. Please greet your parents, your sisters, and your brother Heinz in particular.

Loving you in the Lord with unending happiness,
your loyal Ebbo

Halle
February 27, 1908

My Ebbo,

Your sweet letter came today and gave me great joy. It's hard for me to accept that you won't be here before the 29th, but I understand why, and if Jesus doesn't want you to arrive earlier, then I don't either.

What you write about our future is beautiful. I, too, believe God will lead us wonderfully even if our parents make things difficult for us. They've often said that they'll never consent to our marriage until you have a secure position, but I'm not going to let their disapproval prevent me from doing what seems to me to be God's will. *God* led us together and will therefore continue to lead us, so we can't possibly let ourselves be influenced by what is pleasing or displeasing to our parents. I've told mine this often. And if we have God on our side, we can be completely confident, my dearest.

Yesterday was a very sobering day for me: In the morning I went to the funeral of a dear believer, a sister in the Lord who had led many people to Jesus. She was only thirty years old, or so. A brother of hers conducted the burial, and Pastor Hobbing spoke on the text, "We bless those who are chosen."

Later, in the afternoon, I went to another funeral, this time for a twenty-two-year-old sister from the Union. She had been converted a few years ago and had led many to Jesus since then. For the last half year, however, she suffered from mental illness and considered herself cursed by God. It always seemed to help when Fräulein Sack talked with her, which she did often. On the second day of Christmas she went to Pastor Hobbing and told him that Christmas was her wedding and her bridegroom was not of this world. Following this encounter she went to the river, and was found dead only the day before yesterday. Fräulein Sack wrote me about it, and I went to the funeral for her sake. It was held by Pastor von Bräcker. He said that this was a shaking, mysterious death, in the face of which one can only ask, "Why did this happen?" He also said, "As we gather around this casket, God calls to us, 'Let there be light.'" What are we to learn from this? It was really shattering.

At five o'clock I was asked to go to Fräulein Sack's, and we talked for a long time. She was terribly sad; she said she'd known this young woman in the Union for eight years as a joyful Christian. She was very trusting, however, and said, "I know she is with the Lord."

Fräulein Sack is impressive – an earnest Christian. I love her very much. We first spoke about Jesus and about my attitude to him, and she told me how glad she was that I'd found him. Then she said she'd been asking the Lord for years to show her a way to approach educated young women, and God had now shown her this way in me. She said she hoped that I'd be a blessing to the young women in the Union. I then told her that I'm extremely thankful to him for having placed me in his service, but that I wanted to be completely open with her about everything. Then I told her that I'm convinced about baptism of believers and will act in accordance with my conviction. I assured her that the last thing I want to do is make anyone uneasy by this recognition, or force it on anyone, but that I'd always confess to it. Fräulein Sack was very understanding, and said that she stood for freedom on this point and doesn't want anything except Jesus the crucified to be in the center. I'm very happy that we could speak so openly.

Oh, yes, I wanted to tell you about Pastor Hachtmann's visit too. Apart from one rather impertinent remark, he actually took back all his earlier accusations. And when he dropped some comment about me being untruthful, Papa said, "My children never lie; they're much too proud for that." (Just like Papa!) Then Papa asked them why they were accusing me of anything in the first place, and they said that several times I first denied something and after a while remembered again and admitted it. He said that since he and his wife had never experienced anything like that, they thought I was being untruthful. They said that wouldn't be the worst either, as *every* person tells lies now and then. In response to this Papa said, "Yes, there is a great deal of lying in the world. But my children have always been an exception to that."

Aside from this, I was also somewhat upset because of an impudent remark the Hachtmanns made to Monika. I'm afraid I didn't remain in the spirit of Jesus, but said rather excitedly that I utterly rejected their criticisms. I also told them that they hadn't treated me like a lady, but like a child. At the end of the visit, Pastor Hachtmann tried to arrange for me to return to Brumby, but Mama declined, saying she wanted to keep me at home. That about sums up the visit. Papa isn't too charmed by the Hachtmanns anymore. He only ever liked them because Pastor Hachtmann promised Papa to do all he could to change my convictions about believers' baptism.

I'm sorry about many things from my time in Brumby – but if a child of God cannot live according to her conscience, it's worse than physical pain. I never told them a *conscious* lie, though several times I realized afterward that something I'd said wasn't quite true. In every case I went and told them this, as you know. This experience was humiliating, but I'm still thankful for it. I'm also grateful that God gave me a sharp conscience with regard to lying.

I'll close now so I can mail this letter. Jesus protect you, my only darling. Let people think what they want, as long as we can remain in him.

Loving you endlessly in him,
your faithful Emmy

Papa and Mama keep saying that they're going to write you.

Breslau
March 1, 1908

Daniel 10:12: "Do not be afraid, Daniel. Since the first day that you set your mind to gain understanding and to humble yourself before your God, your words were heard, and I have come in response to them."

Beloved Emmy,

I feel so full of the spirit of prayer that I could spend a whole day imploring that God be honored and we all might be saved and purified and healed. The Book of Daniel, which I just finished reading today for the second time, has made a very powerful impression on me, especially Daniel's prayer in chapter 9, and the angel's answer in 10:12.

I've experienced a lot inwardly and want to write you about everything as far as this is possible. First, I'm starting on the five Books of Moses tomorrow and will read seven chapters every day. At that rate, I'll finish on March 28, and then we can discuss the continuation of our reading. The prescriptions of the Law don't apply to us *at all* anymore, so the important thing is to understand them in context, and to discern in them the deeper meaning that points to the New Covenant. One needs the Holy Spirit to accomplish this.

I'm upset with myself for having been so *stupid* as to send you a parcel yesterday. I should have remembered that they aren't delivered on Sundays anymore. All the more, I thank *you* for your precious Sunday letter, which made me extremely happy and strengthened me. I read a part of it in church, before taking part in the Lord's Supper, and was deeply blessed by it. I felt so powerfully the holiness and strength of God and the indwelling spirit of Jesus, the crucified. At the same time I was terribly weighed down by the heaviness of attending the Lord's Supper with my parents. Papa told me very earnestly yesterday that if I ever get baptized I'd be as bad as, or worse than, an atheist to him.

You know, dear Emmy, I never want to be found a condemning judge (Matthew 7:1–5). I pray for those who are dear to me with all seriousness and faith, and know that I am a sinner myself, but I can't close my eyes to the fact that they represent the most terrible self-delusion and hypocrisy. This humbles me and makes me pray fervently that they may be saved and completely healed. I, too, want to be redeemed from all hypocrisy, all pretense, all sin. Oh, that we might fall on our faces like Daniel and beg expiation for our sins and for the sin of all people!

My parents have finally begun to do battle in earnest against my conviction about baptism. We had some difficult conversations in which I was quite forceful, and I'm afraid I got rather passionate at times. Last night, however, I was able to tell Papa that Jesus would keep me calm in our discussions. He has blessed me so deeply and assured me of his strength as the indwelling Christ. As to the question of my future profession, my parents are already beginning to back down, even if the facts are not to their liking. If I'm not baptized, they will, with the help of your parents, do everything they can to force me into taking the second state exam and into the service of the church. But this would mean not only a divergence from my life's divine calling, and a warping of my inner character, but could also result in the postponement of our wedding for *years*. Once I'm baptized, however, they will no longer be able to force me into this and will only press for a secure position with the fellowship – something I can agree with. Because of their anxiety over all this, they've turned sharply against baptism and are now trying to get me to go to Hänisch's bible class, making jokes about my "social demise," declaring baptism to be the greatest sin, and saying that they'll have to disown us both, fully and forever.

All this is actually happening rather quietly, for the most part, and giving me ample opportunities to prove my love and steadfastness. I pray, and I am happy. My parents' threats don't mean much to me, since I'm quite sure that in the long run there won't be any essential change in our relationship. Things will cool off. As the saying goes, "You don't eat soup as hot as you cook it." The main thing is to stay as calm as possible and politely put off discussions about the future for as long as we can.

We'll have to fight for ourselves, certainly – but I already have. I spoke my piece very clearly last year on March 29 about my future prospects and didn't meet any significant opposition. Besides, in Papa's letter he wrote, "Should you then, after passing your Ph.D. exam, find a secure position as preacher of your fellowship, I would not be able to place any obstacle in the way of your being united in marriage." Well, I'm completely in agreement with this and will just need to remind Papa, as a man of honor, to keep his word.

In the meantime, I really don't think we need to worry about getting married amid protests from our parents. On the contrary, I have every hope for a harmonious wedding, and we should pray for this. May God grant it soon.

I've finished cramming church history now (that is, my *first* review of it), so next week I'll work on my exam application and get through the necessary arrangements and interviews. At the same time, however, I want to read some more things on church history and review my Hebrew, and by March 28 I want to complete the first Old Testament review. From March 31 on I'll get down to my written work and the translations from the Old and New Testaments. I really need more practice in that. I also want to get through the history of philosophy and symbolism for the first time by the end of June, so as to have the time from July to October completely free for reviewing material already learned. During Easter week in Halle, I plan to put in four hours of studying a day.

Pray hard, dear Emmy, that God gives me strength, because failure is completely out of the question.

Your faithful Ebbo

Halle
March 7, 1908

2 Corinthians 3:17–18: "Now the Lord is the Spirit, and where the Spirit of the Lord is, there is freedom. And we, who with unveiled faces all reflect the Lord's glory, are being transformed into his likeness with ever-increasing glory, which comes from the Lord, who is the Spirit."

My dear Ebbo,

I have a good half hour to write to you now, though that's not much.

I've been reading seven chapters from the Books of Moses every day and am managing that. I'm amazed at everything *you* accomplish! I like the Elberfeld Bible – it's so much easier to understand than other translations. Yesterday afternoon at four I went to a very good bible study with Kühn in the new Alliance Hall. He spoke about Romans 8, from verse 18 to the end. I think it's just marvelous: "I consider that our present sufferings are not worth comparing with the glory that will be revealed in us." Kühn spoke magnificently about God's plan and about Christ and his church.

Afterward, Frau Baehr and I went home together. She told me she was sorry that I was active in the Young Women's Union, since there's still so much that's "unclear" there. I admitted that this was true, but pointed out that there are young women in the Union who are indeed sisters in Jesus, that I must utilize my free time for him so that I don't backslide, and that at the moment this activity is all that's available to me. Frau Baehr assured me that she also loved these sisters but still didn't think that this work was good for a new convert. She's extremely nice, but I do find her somewhat one-sided. Yes, there are Christians who are unclear on this and that, yet they can still be very close to Jesus, and I've gotten to know quite a number of people like this. I guess I'm still not decided on this issue. I'm certain, though, that God will lead me and show me what he wants.

Evangelist Veller is coming this evening and will be here for two weeks. We distributed about fifty invitations for him in the vocational school today. The theme of his lecture series is, "The Greatest Evil in the World." I'm going to Frau Dr. Schulze's for a bible class now, and tomorrow looks like it will be just as busy. I'm so happy I can use my time for Jesus. If only something comes out of it for him! I'm going to pray very hard that your work and time are also utilized completely for Jesus.

I've just returned from Frau Dr. Schulze's, where ten of us gathered today. It's marvelous how God is working there. Fräulein Seligmüller and a Frau Pastor Knack were present too.

We spoke about Luke 19. I think I'll speak about Colossians 3 next time. Most of those who came weren't wholly converted.

I must close. May God bless your meeting in Brockau tomorrow, as well as the evangelization work here. Pray that I always look to him and never to myself. When I look at myself, I often feel I will fail, but thanks to God, he is our peace.

Your loving bride

Breslau
March 8, 1908

Emmy, my sweet,

Since I got back from Brockau early, there's still time to write to you. Today I saw that the Enemy is especially active there. Some of the older members are in great danger of letting go of Jesus. Pray that God may come into his own all the more there, and come to victory. Faith moves mountains.

Your letter made me tremendously happy. (By the way, don't forget Papa's birthday on Tuesday.) It's very loving of you to read seven chapters every day. It's actually so easy, and you can only receive true blessing from reading larger amounts. Smaller snippets, read by themselves, can often leave one confused. Have you caught up to me, then? Today I finished all but one chapter of Genesis. I always read the underlined passages again in Luther's version. By the way, I wouldn't put your Luther Bible away, but use both that and the Elberfeld translation whenever you can.

I'm terrifically happy you are using your time for Jesus. That's just what I want for myself. May God give you an active prayer life and the Holy Spirit, so that you can win many people for eternity.

I rejoice that you've found fulfillment in the Union without provoking irritating conflicts at home. I'm also glad you're getting to know all kinds of Christians and thus will never be tempted to judge people by externals.

However, I can understand Frau Baehr's worry that constant contact with certain circles might lead you to belittle your own scriptural recognitions. Christians think so differently, and one might easily get accustomed to a Christianity that esteems only those truths that are recognized by all. We can't accept this sort of ecumenism. And we must also seek to grow in grace and recognition and not just settle for what we've already experienced. Colossians 4:12, etc. We'll soon be able to have a good talk about all this.

It's only natural that Christians who are unclear about many things can still be close to Jesus, since grace depends only on the heart, and new recognitions don't bring new levels of salvation, but new responsibilities. It remains, however, that in 2 Peter 3:18 it says, "Grow in grace *and* knowledge." The body of Christ can never move forward and will never be made ready for the goal if everybody remains on the same level of understanding and action out of a false alliance. But stay calm: you're still young in Christ, and he will lead you wonderfully.

Still, I think it is important to allow yourself to be made ready, so that you'll be able to understand me and come with me in taking steps that have enormous import for God's kingdom.

We both have, through God, a great responsibility as to the unfolding history of his kingdom and its development toward the final goal, a responsibility that goes beyond the winning of hearts and having fellowship with the saved, because it presupposes and includes both of these things. I actually believe that the Union can't give this to you and could even take it away without your wanting it. You'll understand me when we talk about it.

For the time being keep working faithfully in the Union and wherever else you can, and keep in close contact with *all*, not least with the Alliance Hall. Study the Bible thoroughly and pray for grace and knowledge. I'm going to do the same, and God will help us keep pace with one another.

I'm very happy to be fully occupied with studying. Tomorrow I hope to send off my exam application. But now it's time to close, my darling. May God give you many blessings in the Union and everywhere. I rejoice in your activities there, and I give thanks and pray for you.

Remember me, too, so that I may conquer in everything and constantly be full of joy in Jesus.

I love you boundlessly, with fullest dedication and joy, and I look forward immensely to seeing you in three weeks. May Jesus protect you with his joy and his peace.

Your faithful Ebbo

Excuse the appearance of this letter. I wrote it standing up. Jesus be with you and with me!

Emmy's lack of a response to Eberhard's thoughts on God's kingdom, and to his concerns about her activities in the Young Women's Union, troubled him. He wrote that he'd expected at least some sort of reaction when such important subjects were on the table. She apologized, but said she couldn't understand why he and others in the movement would question her activities, as long as her conscience wasn't bothered by it.

Halle
April 11, 1908

John 3:36: "Whoever has the Son has eternal life!"

My Ebbo,

I've been staying home a lot these rainy days, mostly dressmaking. I'm also reading *The Great Struggle,* your copy of *Advice for the Saving of Souls,* and a great deal from the Bible. In the mornings I've been reading Matthew. Today I read chapter 10 (on my own) and then the Letter to the Corinthians with Heinz. In the evenings my sisters and I are reading the Revelation of John together, and I'm continuing in the Old Testament as well. I haven't finished Joshua yet. It's much more wonderful when you read these things two or three times. It's too much to absorb in only one read.

I'm looking forward tremendously to a week from today when you'll come and we can discuss everything again, and to Easter, and to praying often together. Many thanks for the little card and for the sweet violets. Heinz greets you very warmly, by the way. He's attending Passion devotions at the Catholic Church every Friday now. When I told Mama about this recently, she said she'd much rather have that than see us get baptized, since going to a Catholic Church at least doesn't involve despising the sacrament. She also says we ought to realize that leaving the church means committing perjury, since at confirmation one promises to be true to the church forever. It's really remarkable how the devil tries to stop serious Christians from following Jesus all the way.

But we must bring all these concerns to him! John 16:12 has become very important for me, especially in the work for souls: "I have much more to say to you, more than you can now bear." Often it seems that there's so much they don't understand, and yet they *do* have life from God. That's surely how it is with me, too, in many things. And so one has to simply let things grow. If one is always forced, like a plant in a greenhouse, the new life one receives will not really be a fruit of the Spirit. It was dangerous how much weight I put on the opinions of other Christians. I even began to feel that I myself didn't have to decide about matters like the Lord's Supper. It's pretty clear to me now, from reading the Bible, that I can't take part in it at church anymore, mostly because the pastor pronounces the forgiveness of sins as he celebrates communion (I haven't read *anything* to back that up), and furthermore because unbelievers share in it.

Earlier I thought I'd stop going simply because the more serious Christians in our church were no longer taking part. But that's terrible. Perhaps now you'll see why I don't want to listen to what people say about the Union. Of course, if you really want me to withdraw from it, I'll do it – I wouldn't have any joy in it anymore. I haven't been there since Sunday anyway. On the other hand, my darling, I just can't understand why you're so concerned and don't trust that Jesus will guide me. The *surest* recognition about something like this comes from the Bible, after all, and not from having an opinion stuffed down one's throat. You've never done that so far, of course. But I don't think it would be right to withdraw without being personally convinced about it. How would I explain it to Jesus? That I was afraid of becoming superficial?

I must close, however. I'll write more on Monday. May Jesus protect you.

Loving you in him,
your faithful Emmy

Breslau
April 12, 1908

Romans 8:32: "He who did not spare his own Son, but gave him up for us all – how will he not also, along with him, graciously give us all things?"

My only and infinitely beloved bride,

Never yet have I prayed over a letter as I did today. It pains me that the Enemy has brought you into such unrest about the Union and my attitude to it. I can't ask you enough to forgive me for not having spoken more fully in Jesus' spirit on my last visit. If I had, I wouldn't have expressed myself so awkwardly, and you would not have misunderstood me as you seem to have. When we're together again, let's humble ourselves and ask God that we never distress each other so deeply again.

Now to the point: You yourself know that a year ago you could only understand a small part of my biblical range of thoughts. That hasn't changed, and I feel I can't burden you yet with everything that the Lord has laid upon me. To me, there's nothing more horrible than pushing one's ideas on others before their recognition matures independently. I hate and reject such a violation of the bud; that's why I'm deeply troubled that, without wanting or knowing it, I hurt you in just this way.

You know how I've always implored you to hold to *no one,* and to be guided by *nothing,* but *Jesus alone,* as he reveals himself to you every day. We must never retreat from this rock by so much as one millimeter. That's why it's completely out of the question that I'd ever tell you to withdraw from the Union. How can you even write such nonsense (I mean "nonsense" in the sense of "impossibility")! If anything, it's my greatest wish that you might continue to work diligently and energetically in the Union, with burning joy and love for each immortal soul. This is *his work* after all, and you must go at it with new energy.

Even though you worry (and I understand) that the unequivocal clarity of Christ might be obscured for you in the Union – because lines that they perceive to be too sharp are softened, and important and decisive demands are weakened by being applied to individual cases only and not to all Christians – you should never allow that to frighten you from the Union. Rather, it should spur you on to embrace and proclaim the Lord all the more clearly, wherever this is needed.

There's only one reason for withdrawing from such an association: when your conscience is violated – when you're required to do something you consider wrong – or when through mere membership you support, confess, and defend something you consider unbiblical and objectionable. As you don't seem to have this conviction, a withdrawal would be a sin against yourself and against the body of Christ.

My sweetest: I'm really not at all worried about your inner development and the influence of the Union. I have too much trust in Jesus and in the perfection of our mutual relationship for that, and I know we'll be led to the same understanding. But even if I'm not worried, it remains my duty to alert you to the dangers I see, even if you don't see them yet.

John 16:12 must not be taken too far. It must be understood only insofar that we don't force things upon others out of our own strength. Look at the context of this verse: it merely leads up to verse 13. This Spirit has been poured out, and the whole of truth revealed, for each one. Certainly, the devil always places obstacles in the way – this one for this person and that one for another. Yet the whole truth is there, in the Word, for everyone. And it must therefore be proclaimed to everyone, in the Holy Spirit. It's a false, dangerous teaching to think that one believer must not influence another in his development, that each must follow his own leading, that the Lord shows one person this and another person that, that the other person is right, too, but has just been led differently.

Emmy, this is one of the greatest dangers that exists in our circles: the danger of mystical subjectivism. And combating it is one of the most important life-tasks I have set for myself. It is a false way, horrible even, because it sounds so plausible. Some go so far as to say that one must never demand of anyone else that he subordinate himself to a particular word of scripture, since one doesn't know whether the Spirit has made it important to him. Such people argue that only those words of the Bible are important which the Spirit has made "living" for them. This is sentimental and unrealistic; it is a mystical subjectivism that does not permit the whole truth of scripture to prevail, but only the feelings and inclinations of the individual Christian.

In opposition to this, we must promote biblically realistic objectivism. Let us testify, with Jesus, to John 16:13: "He will guide you into all truth!" For us, at least, he is here right now, through the writings of the apostles – his complete revelation. There is no more waiting.

We have the whole truth in the Word. And it holds true for every person, immediately and completely. Not only when a verse or passage has been made "important and wonderful" for one, but always. And if a believer does not understand something, then we may, paraphrasing John 16:12, surmise that he is not yet far enough along to grasp it and does not possess the Spirit.

For the Spirit *does* exist and can and will lead the Christian to perfect clarity again and again. And so we must humble ourselves if we so often have the miserable kind of conversions where everything is so unclear – they're exactly what the devil wants.

What we really need is to pray with the person concerned, and show him what is lacking, so that he may surrender himself fully and completely. Mostly that is what is lacking: absolute dedication. Because when it is present, it results in the most staggeringly clear understanding.

But I have digressed. Emmy, I am so happy that you are having so many experiences in Halle; and I am thankful that through the Union you are getting acquainted with city mission work, despite the fact that it was the venture that pleased me the least in Halle, as it seemed the furthest removed from biblical clarity and power. Should I turn out to be deluded in thinking this, I shall be glad to be corrected.

It's by virtue of the fact that we develop independently in Jesus that we learn the most from each other. I owe a tremendously great deal to your initial feeling and understanding of divine things. So it is my earnest desire that God lead you onward quite freely to a more complete understanding of his Son. As for your activity and development in the Union, I joyously and gratefully commend it to the Lord. I, too, would like to further and strengthen it – not prevent and hinder it. It was right of me to call your attention to its dangers, as I have always done and will always do. But now the Lord must lead you through all the spiritual currents and streams of knowledge that could so easily confuse and distract a young child of God. In him is our trust!

Above all, it gives me endless joy that you desire to save all who can be saved. O beloved Emmy, may the devil never rob you of this fire of the Holy Spirit that leaves us no rest until one lost person after another is safe. Think on it, Jesus wants you to bear fruit in the service of God – and so do I – so that saving souls becomes your passion, your happiness! Saving souls, the rebirth of human hearts, stands above everything else when you think of hell, or of the kingdom of heaven. There are higher points of view, such as the honor of God, the preparation of the church for its returning king, and similar matters. But this is the first, the most basic thing. I would therefore advise you that as long as you cannot do it elsewhere, by all means carry on your work of saving souls in the Union, even if, for the sake of your conscience, you do not feel able to become a member.

Believe me: all I wanted was that in the midst of your work you should take care not to lose clarity in your thinking. Go on working, stay alert, and object to anything that is obviously wrong, and refrain from taking part in it. Finally, remember that the unity of the body of Christ, in love and in the common witness of grace, is one of the most important possessions of the church on earth. Therefore I rejoice when you show love and loyalty to every kind of Christian, and testify and try to win people for Jesus from all backgrounds insofar as your conscience allows you.

I would gladly tell you about my studies, but time is passing by too fast. I have to leave right away for Brockau. The main thing and the most glorious is that we will soon be seeing one another and will be able to talk everything over thoroughly.

Main Station
April 12, 1908

In Brockau today I spoke on John 16:7–14, about the Holy Spirit. Jesus gave me great joy and assurance, and I spoke with burning enthusiasm. It is nearly eleven o'clock now, and I must go home so as to be fresh tomorrow.

Jesus protect you, my delightful little bird. My love for you is deeper than the ocean, wider than all worlds, higher than all heavens, hotter than all suns, truer and finer than anything else in me. You, Emmy, are my happiness and my delight, my life and my being. You are everything to me in Jesus, our Lord, to whom we belong wholly and totally!

Looking forward,
your loving Eberhard

The Light of God

During the Easter break, Eberhard and Emmy spent many hours together. One result was Emmy's decision to withdraw from the Union: she decided that as long as she was forbidden to voice her criticisms of the state church, there was no point in staying there. Eberhard encouraged her, however, to continue meeting informally with the young women she'd gotten to know and to guide as many as possible toward conversion. The next month, May, was difficult for the von Hollanders: first Monika and then Else became gravely ill. Meanwhile, Eberhard moved in with the Wiegands, SCM friends in nearby Bebra, with the hope of being able to focus on his studies with fewer interruptions than when in his parents' home.

Halle
June 1, 1908

My dearest Ebbo,

First I must excuse myself for not writing yesterday. In the morning I took part in the Lord's Supper, which was a great blessing. After that there was a prayer meeting for Else's health, lovingly held by brothers and sisters from the movement. (Sister Riedel asked me beforehand if we wanted it.) Oh, and I wanted to tell you that I'm starting to read Romans today.

Yesterday afternoon there was another big ruckus at home. Olga kept needling me – she was annoyed that Else said I was taking good care of her. Then Mama came along and got terribly upset at me, though I hadn't said a word. She said Else's illness was on your and my conscience since *we'd* persuaded her to be baptized. She called us re-baptizers and said she'll be glad to see the day when I leave the house – the sooner the better. This morning she isn't speaking to me, and acting as if I've deeply offended her (I told her last night that her accusations were made up). I would gladly have left the house immediately, but that would have distressed Else no end. Monika and Heinz, who were present during the whole affair, are wholly on my side and extremely indignant about this injustice. Papa also says he can't understand how a mother can snub her child like she did me, and say such unbelievable things to her. Of course, it's really all Olga's fault again. She just can't stand it when other people are friendly to me. I'm happy to overlook what Mama said to me, though if she says anything about you I won't take it. It seems it would be best for me to spend this summer somewhere else, though it will be difficult to organize. The Lord can't be sending us all these experiences for nothing.

Yesterday afternoon I was planning to attend a baptism at four o'clock, but never got there. In the evening, though, I went to a wonderful meeting held by Brother Steinhardt, on Acts 10, and didn't get home until almost eleven o'clock.

I'm glad that you're well and happy and that you had such a fine Sunday. Everyone sends you warm greetings, and Else in particular thanks you for the flowers. She's about the same. Brother Stenzel led a fine prayer meeting with her yesterday, and Mama was there too. I must close now. I'm looking forward very eagerly to your coming. Maybe we can go out for the whole day, if the weather is nice. By the way, *don't* write to my parents about yesterday's incident. Just act as if nothing happened, otherwise there'll be another big scene. Papa is actually pretty friendly. Maybe it will all blow over.

Yours faithfully, Emmy

Bebra
June 2, 1908

1 Peter 2:19–23: "It is commendable if a man bears up under the pain of unjust suffering because he is conscious of God. But how is it to your credit if you receive a beating for doing wrong and endure it? But if you suffer for doing good and you endure it, this is commendable before God. To this you were called, because Christ suffered for you, leaving you an example, that you should follow in his steps. 'He committed no sin, and no deceit was found in his mouth.' When they hurled their insults at him, he did not retaliate; when he suffered, he made no threats. Instead, he entrusted himself to him who judges justly."

My sweet, dear Emmy,

Reading your letter made me so upset and indignant that I wanted to let Olga feel the effects of her meanness to the full by refusing to enter your parents' house again without a special invitation. I soon realized, however, that my anger was from the devil, and prayed for the spirit of him who suffered more than any and was yet without sin, unlike us.

It then became clear to me that we should feel *sorry* for Olga, that she is capable of acting so nastily and that she is so quarrelsome and disunited, poor thing, while we are so over-abundantly rich in blessings. The situation isn't too different with your Mama, even if she is more innocent and less calculating in her wrongdoing and sin. I'm sure she knows in her heart of hearts that these reproaches don't apply to us. If she really wished death on herself and Else while calling on God's holy name, that's very serious. God won't forget this, unless she is reborn through the blood of Jesus. It makes me feel that we must have a warmer, deeper compassion for these dear, unhappy souls who are, on top of it all, our nearest blood relatives; and we must show them love tenfold, yes hundredfold if we are able. May the Lord save us from all family politics so that we're always prepared to tell them, especially Olga, how desperate their condition is.

In general, I wouldn't take such family scenes too seriously, since unconverted people don't usually mean what they say and are used to giving free rein to their whims. In cases like this it might be best to go outdoors and avoid such things as much as possible. After a few days, Mama and Olga will be friendly to you again. An unconverted person just is filled with discord, because he or she is continually pulled this way and that by evil. We should give thanks all the more whenever such a one makes attempts to be good.

I think it would be better, though, if we chose somewhere outside Halle the next time we meet. What about Weimar or Eisenach? By the way, tell Mama that unfortunately the honor and grace of having convinced Else of the biblical truth she has embraced with regard to baptism doesn't belong to us: sad to say, we recognized it much later than she. Greet everyone, especially Else! We're praying for her often.

Your Ebbo

Removed from the commotion that marked life at his parents' house, Eberhard was happy for a quiet place to work, and his studies progressed rapidly. He saw Emmy several times over the summer, and both of them continued to write to each other daily. In mid-July, the couple met in Halle after an incident involving Lucia Franke's father. Neither Eberhard's nor Emmy's letters go into detail, but this much is clear: Herr Franke accused Eberhard of having treated his daughter dishonorably, and attempted to turn the von Hollanders against him. Eberhard refused to fight back or insist on his innocence, and instead, decided to use the painful predicament as an opportunity for self-examination.

Halle
July 11, 1908

Romans 12:1–2: "I urge you, brothers, in view of God's mercy, to offer your bodies as living sacrifices, holy and pleasing to God – this is your spiritual act of worship. Do not conform any longer to the pattern of this world, but be transformed by the renewing of your mind. Then you will be able to test and approve what God's will is – his good, pleasing and perfect will."

1 John 3:19–20: "This then is how we know that we belong to the truth, and how we set our hearts at rest in his presence whenever our hearts condemn us. For God is greater than our hearts, and he knows everything."

My dearest Ebbo,

It is very distressing to me how God has had to humble us in the past days. But I have certainty that through prayer we will be freed more fully than ever before! It's a shame we haven't utilized the gifts he gave us in one another, and that we didn't always use the time we had together to help each other along. This must change completely from now on. I'm going to pray constantly for you and your studies, for your final exam, and for your future vocation, that God gives you everything you need. We can only stand in awe before God's omnipotence and before his holiness, which won't tolerate the slightest degree of devilry. We ought to sacrifice ourselves in everything, come what may. I feel so unworthy and weak, but he will help us. And let us keep reminding each other what we've really known all the time: that our bond *is with the Father and in his son Jesus Christ.*

Loving you eternally in the Lord,
your faithful Emmy

P.S. Do you think I might be able to approach Lucia Franke somehow, maybe through others in the movement?

Bebra
July 12, 1908

Beloved bride of my heart,

I've never approached anything so solemnly, but that's good. It seems God is at last going deep with me, and I want to submit quietly to him, so that my surrender is a living, holy sacrifice. You'll reply that then there's really no reason to be sad. But one thing grieves me persistently: that when I took leave of you, I made you so sad, my darling. Please forgive me. Above all let nothing make you depressed or unnatural. It would be too awful if the great gift of your gracious and innocent joy were lost or weakened. It's just what I need when faced with the terrible seriousness of life. I firmly believe that the experiences of our time and the power of the Word will bring us to the point where we can be completely joyful, and yet have, simultaneously, a deep, well-rounded discernment for the great tasks of the kingdom.

It hurts me deeply that I caused you such great distress, but that's how it must be since we're completely one. But it is *I* who have sinned. *I* have been unfaithful to the Lord. *I* denied his spirit. *I* was increasingly rebellious. I'm entirely unworthy of God's grace and of his gifts, and also unworthy of you, my darling.

But Jesus is greater. *Jesus is greater!* He bursts all chains and makes us completely free. Let us live solely, exclusively, fully, and deeply for him alone. Not for our principles, ethics, and nobility of feeling. *Only for him.* Let us regard *everything* else as dirt in order to win Christ. That's what Paul said, and by that he meant even high-minded, pious scholarship and zealous morality. *Jesus alone!* Only in him can we be holy, and thus pure and happy, strong and rich. No one can weaken us, nothing can cripple us when we have Jesus alone.

Jesus alone! It is in this sense that we are engaged; *this* is our relationship. Herein rests our love. It is the strength of our happiness, the goal of our loving. *Jesus alone!* Thus I love you and live for you, and remain yours from everlasting to everlasting.

Your faithful old Ebbo

There's one more thing I have to confess: I told you once that I always wore a certain kind of garment. That wasn't true. I always *wanted* to wear something like it, but didn't actually have one at that time. It's humbling to admit this, but I'm very sorry I lied to you like that. It definitely won't happen again. (I'm trying to think whether it's happened other times too!) The light of God is so clear and serious.

Bebra
July 12, 1908

My one and only Emmy,

My heart is still so full that I could write pages and pages to you. But it's already evening, and I want to be fresh for work tomorrow. It's good I traveled on Saturday; I was so dead tired from everything that, apart from some letters and tidying up, I had to rest both days. (That's why I didn't take the book *Kingdom Songs* to the station with the letter until late Saturday. But you've surely received it by now. I hope there was no overdue postage to pay. It was under 250 grams.)

Today we read 2 Corinthians 6, and I prayed over it very earnestly. I shall do so still more. I've been praying a lot generally and thinking things over quite seriously, and the Lord has shown me in various ways that he desires to bless me.

The silence here has done me a world of good. This morning we had a marvelous meeting about Genesis 18, on what God wants of us: 1) honesty about our sins (verse 15), 2) faith in the promises of God (verse 14), and 3) prayers that the lost world be saved (verse 32).

In regard to 1), I would like to tell you once again that I am so ashamed about the whole situation with the Frankes. Despite everything, I must recognize my role at that time as sinful, and that pains me terribly. Let me refer you to last year's letters. Herr Franke is right: my conduct at that time did not correspond to my words, even though I wanted it to. I wish I'd also written to the Frankes, "I thank you very much for having forgiven me the mistakes of my inexperience." I did *say* it. As for 2), let us hold fast, my darling. God forgives and saves fully; he has power to make everything new. I believe it. And for this reason he will also give us, more and more, the strength for 3).

In retrospect, I'm sorry you didn't pass on the letter I wrote to your parents; that was surely not right. But let us now proceed with heroic courage, with Jesus, fearing nothing. Today at our meeting we sang, "Stand up!" and "The life of bliss."

Your loving letter gave me infinitely much. Write like that as often as you can. You are right: we must change completely and begin our engagement all over again, in a certain way. Praise God that he forgives us, and that you've forgiven me too.

Eternally thankful for your faithful help and great love, and unworthy of you, but full of trust,

your forever loving Eberhard

Greet your parents, especially Papa, and all your sisters, and your brother too. I have no stamps, and everyone has gone to bed. I'll have to mail this tomorrow.

Halle
July 13, 1908

What joy to be nothing, yes, nothing,
   although it will cut my own flesh.
I'll gladly be low and humble
   if Jesus is seen all afresh.
Not I, but he above all things –
   see then how pure blessings will flow.
O raise then your voices, rejoicing,
   to honor and praise him alone.

2 Thessalonians 2:14: "He called you to this through our gospel, that you might share in the glory of our Lord Jesus Christ."

My beloved Eberhard,

My warmest thanks for both of your letters and for the charming little book of *Kingdom Songs.* I, too, pray that God will give me a deeper understanding for his great thoughts. I'm still unhappy about what happened. I have a somewhat different take on the whole thing, but I won't worry about it anymore, so long as the Spirit makes it clear to you.

I'm just reading an excellent book by a true man of God, Fränkel, and feel so blessed by it.

I'm very encouraged by the thought, "He who is in you is greater than the one who is in the world (1 John 4:4)." We need to *experience* this truth.

I talked with Monika yesterday, and she openly told me she'd never really been converted, only "moved," though had often prided herself on having had a conversion. She said she just can't turn her back on the world: it is too noble and too beautiful. She says she wants to enjoy life, and that serious Christians are misguided and tactless. She said the last straw was the evening with Lucia Franke. I told her she'd be eternally lost if she rejected the Lord, but she said she found the tensions at home and elsewhere too great to be willing to take them upon herself for a cause she can't even believe in wholeheartedly. She said she respects our convictions, but can't join us in holding them herself. She then begged me very ardently not to let ourselves be separated, saying she loves us too much. I simply replied that it made me sad that she was rejecting Jesus. I'm going to give her the letter from you later. We need to use every opportunity to tell her about Jesus and to pray for her.

Papa and Mama are going to invite you for your birthday. Let's pray that we use it in such a way that it blesses us and our family. I must close, however, my Ebbo. Jesus be with you. May he give you strength so that *everything* you do, say, and think is to his honor alone. I wish the same for myself. Only in that way will we be completely one in Jesus.

Yours deeply in love, Emmy

Toward the end of the summer, Emmy developed a severe sinus inflammation. Given the state of medicine at that time – illnesses that are easily treatable today were often fatal then – her condition was taken very seriously.

Halle
July 28, 1908

My beloved Ebbo,

This morning I visited Professor Schwartze. He advises the same as Dr. Herrschel. He treated me today and wants to repeat the treatment on Thursday. He hopes an operation won't be necessary, although he thinks it probably will be. It wasn't really necessary for me to see him since he said exactly the same thing as Herrschel. If I had a say in it, I'd wait until next year before having anything done. The two days you spent here were wonderful – I'm especially happy we could celebrate your birthday together.

In deep love,
your bride

Bebra
July 29, 1908

Psalm 28:7: "The Lord is my strength and my shield."

My beloved, darling bride,

Praise and thanks to God that we're both so fully in him that we're ready to bear everything he sends us. Let us always move forward, so that Jesus becomes greater for us and his name may be ever more glorious through us. If we're on fire with his love, we'll be victorious over every danger.

Emmy, I'm more and more concerned about your illness and am glad you're not the one who has to decide about it. That nonsense you wrote about waiting till next year is out of the question.

I wish I could trust you not to influence Schwartze to settle for a mediocre cure instead of the best. And I'm very sorry you considered going to the Patows when what you need is a time of rest, and that you write, "It wouldn't exactly need to be the shore." This only confirms my apprehension that you might, out of false considerations, attempt to shortchange yourself with regard to the attention that your health (and therefore your bridegroom!) most decidedly demands.

Please, dear Emmy, show me your true love by telling Schwartze that the very best must be done for you. If, for example, you need to go to Italy in the winter to recuperate, tell him that this will be seen to immediately, as a matter of course. I mention this only as an example so that you can see there are no bounds for me when your well-being is at stake.

If the operation can be avoided, of course I'll be extremely thankful, since I don't consider it without danger because of the proximity to the brain. If it can't be avoided, however, then we cannot postpone it, and I'll come to Halle to be with you. In the meantime, I know that God will protect you and therefore I'm not worried.

Your infinitely and eternally loving Ebbo

Langeoog

Else's baptism took place on August 2, 1908, in the following manner: Because she had repeatedly defied her parents by stating her intention to be baptized in spite of their opposition, Herr von Hollander locked her in a third-floor room. As she sat by the window looking out over the city, she saw a rainbow above the Saale River and took it as a sign that a baptism was being held there. Trying the supposedly locked door, she found it open and hurried down to the river, where she met a baptismal procession, joined it, and was baptized. Returning home with soaking clothes and dripping hair, she was startled to see both of her parents and her sister Olga coming down the street. Else braced herself for the impending explosion and continued walking toward them, but when they crossed paths, it was as if they were blind: they did not even notice her.

Writing to Eberhard the same day, Emmy said, "Our parents have no idea what happened; everything went very well. Now Else's going to wait for a suitable moment to tell them." All the same, it was obvious that a family crisis was imminent. Eberhard, determined to remove Emmy from a strenuous situation that might further endanger her health, used money from a small inheritance to rent a room for her in a spa on Langeoog, a North Sea island popular with vacationers. Meanwhile, he found himself having to resolve a headache-inducing misunderstanding with Ludwig von Gerdtell.

Bebra
August 8, 1908

Best beloved Emmy,

You'll have wondered, precious darling, why I've only sent telegrams and flowers since you left Halle. Hopefully they've been sufficient to show you how much I love you and think of you. There are several reasons I haven't had time for a longer letter. Above all, the situation with my doctoral exam has come to a head and is making extraordinary demands on me; secondly, some discussions with von Gerdtell are taking up a lot of my time and strength. I'll have to go to Breslau for a few days tomorrow, or the day after at the latest, to see what can still be done about my exam. What happened is that Church Councilor Genrich spent some time with Papa, and the two of them spoke about my intention to be baptized. Papa told him I'll never have myself baptized, but for truthfulness' sake, I felt I had to add to my application to the Council a note advising them that after my final exam I would withdraw from the church by taking the step of believer's baptism. I did this, and thereupon received letters both from my parents and from Pastor Hänisch requiring me to appear in Breslau for a discussion with the ecclesial authorities. I'll do this with peace and assurance; I know the Lord will care for me and guide everything rightly, truly, and clearly – my trust in him is calm and confident.

As for the matter with von Gerdtell, the same is true. Albert Still stands completely on my side in this conflict and told him his opinion very plainly. I told Ludwig that I'm free from any commitment to them both, now, and consider working together in the future out of the question, as long as he still believes I broke his trust, and might possibly be morally shipwrecked. This was extraordinarily hard for Ludwig, and he kept trying to assure me that he still wants to work with me and doesn't doubt my sincerity or dedication to Christ in the least. Despite my love and esteem for him, however, I think it's a divine leading and grace that I'm free and independent of him now. Self-reliance is the only way to acquire character, after all.

I am well, through God's grace – happy and peaceful in him, and healthy and strong physically. I drove the Wiegand's little horse today for the second time on an outing to a beautiful wood. That's always a lot of fun.

I'm very glad, darling, that you're in Langeoog. I keep thinking, whenever I have a quiet moment, of how you must be enjoying the glorious sea air and the roaring waves that I love so much. It will be very important for you to make some good contacts, too, while you're there. Maybe you can ask the women at the hostel if any of the guests are from fellowship circles. I'm sure you'll get acquainted with the houseguests very quickly, and I can already see you playing boccie after dinner. But most important, go to the beach often, and let the wind blow through you in the sunshine! You ought to consult a spa doctor as well. Tell him about your condition, and ask him whether it's advisable to go swimming. Do this right away; swimming can strengthen you enormously.

Mainly I hope you'll feel better. Never forget that you're on Langeoog *for rest and recuperation.* Naturally you will be glad to witness to others. May some of them be saved! But you should also just enjoy being with them. And stay there a long time, until September 15, if possible.

Always happy when I think of you, because I love you with all the fire of my heart,

I remain your faithful Ebbo

P.S. Rent a little basket chair for yourself for the beach!

Bebra
August 9, 1908

Emmy, my sweet,

I want to tell you why I'm not going to Breslau. It's because I received a telegram saying they're waiving the personal talk I had offered to have with my advisor. So now we must patiently wait for whatever the Lord decides. Should you by any chance receive worrying news from Halle or Breslau about my exam, don't respond to it, and tell them that it's my affair. I'm very happy that you're now in Langeoog and away from all the commotion and hostility. I keep hoping I'll be allowed to sit for the exam, although it's very doubtful now. Naturally, I won't withdraw my application under any circumstances. I'm completely calm about the whole matter, as I am with regard to von Gerdtell too. I could not and cannot act differently. Let us use these days to add to our blessedness and free ourselves more and more from other people's opinions. I'm happy to know that you stand behind me and grateful for your prayers that I follow the Lord, our king, without wavering. Yesterday, by the way, I heard an inspiring sermon by Spurgeon about the faith that overcomes.

Our letters are often held up by the complicated connections to Langeoog. The mail always takes one-and-a-half to two days, and one needs to pay close attention to the departure times of the ships. That's why I sent so many telegrams, which I now want to dispense with.

Please tell me everything you can about the sea, about your contacts, how you are feeling, what your day is like, etc. You can't imagine the joy and comfort your being at the shore gives me. Don't place any limits on your spending under any circumstances, my dear! Buy everything that your health and your convenience require! I doubt you'll have enough money for this, but surely the money I sent will arrive on time. I'm just a bit uneasy that I didn't send enough.

Firm in Jesus,
your Ebbo

When Emmy heard that Eberhard's sister Clara was at a nearby resort, she visited her for a day. While together, the two discussed Eberhard's latest troubles with von Gerdtell.

Bebra
August 21, 1908

I rely on the Lord!

Beloved Emmy,

It's extremely unfortunate that you told Clara about the situation with von Gerdtell. I wonder if Albert wasn't right when he warned me that one should never tell women anything that shouldn't be talked about, since they just can't keep quiet. If that were the case, it would be very sad. Von Gerdtell and I promised one another to be utterly silent about the entire conflict, except to you and Frau von Gerdtell, and to pledge you to silence. I told you this when I was in Halle because I was distressed that Else and Monika already knew about it. And Clara is the kind of person who just isn't able to be silent! Tell her a secret, and she'll repeat it in the most unsuitable place with dramatic embellishments. For this reason, she more than anyone else should never be told what others aren't supposed to know. You didn't by chance also tell her about the Frankes' conduct, did you? And does she realize that von Gerdtell's offense concerns you, among others? Did you tell her what von Gerdtell said about my supposed breach of trust, moral bankruptcy, and lack of character? Dear Emmy, it would be very distressing if you mentioned even one of these points, for in my opinion you would then have sinned, as in James 3:4–5: "Take ships as an example. Although they are so large and are driven by strong winds, they are steered by a very small rudder wherever the pilot wants to go. Likewise the tongue is a small part of the body, but it makes great boasts. Consider what a great forest is set on fire by a small spark." But I don't want to write more about it, since I know how sorry you must be.

Don't think, my dearest, that I want you to be reserved. But haven't we experienced enough to the praise of God and his deeds – so much that we could never finish speaking about it? – that we don't have any time to talk about wrongs and mistakes and injustices? They'll only make us unhappy because they come from the devil. Please, my little Emmy, come to Jesus and tell him, "I rely on you!" I need him much more than you, since I'm much more wretched and despicable, but let's both pray and *believe*. Of course I forgive you and love you very much, as always. But you must pledge Clara to silence immediately, even though she'll probably break it.

And you must stay on Langeoog for as long as your health requires! Imagine, you arrived there only two weeks ago today, and Mama's already asking if you aren't coming home soon! No, my sweetheart, it's my wish that you stay at the resort for five weeks, as long as you continue to enjoy it, and that you not leave the island before September 12. I pray the weather will hold out and be beautiful until then. You'll see to it that you stay in Langeoog until September 12, won't you, my love? And then you should travel home gradually by way of Norderney, Hamburg, Stappenbeck, Salzwedel, and Siedersleben. Don't get home before the first of October. There are various reasons that make this plan desirable:

1) Your absence will generally help your standing at home. The longer you're away, the more they long to have you back.

2) Your recovery will be significantly fuller if you stay longer and travel home slowly. A graduated trip like that, with several days of comfortable stay at each place, is the best follow-up you can have for your cure.

3) The ruckus over Else's baptism doesn't seem to have broken out yet. Until it does, and until it's been dealt with, you cannot possibly go home.

4) The conflicts over my exam will only really begin early September, and I don't want you to be exposed again on any account to the kind of upsets we've unfortunately had to experience several times already.

You'll infer from the enclosed papers that I've had to fight hard in the last weeks. And you'll need to study them in quiet to understand it all. My additional statement about baptism was made necessary by my obligation to be honest, since the Consistory heard from Papa that in his opinion I would never have myself baptized, after a rumor to the opposite effect leaked out from a hostile source. Since the exam presupposes readiness to serve in the church, it would have been hypocrisy and cowardly concealment if I had kept silent under such circumstances. I thank the Lord for preserving me from such dishonest action. It's impossible to foresee what will happen now. The most correct outcome, officially speaking, could be rejection, but it's also very possible that the Consistory will find a different way. Let's pray that only Jesus' perfect will is done, not what we or others wish.

You can imagine that with all this suspense it's impossible to study, particularly since I continually have to answer the kind of letters that solemnly justify the greatest nonsense. In spite of all difficult struggles, however (the hardest being my sinfulness and unworthiness), I feel healthy and have firm confidence that Jesus will guide my and your life in the best and most blessed way. We'll definitely still have to go through many earthly travails, and also through divine suffering, if you think of our own miserableness and of the misery of the many around us who are not saved.

Since I have more time and also need to think over so many serious things, I'm spending a lot of time outdoors in nature and am sending you a few mementos of this today. The photos are from the same outing to Wildeck as the first one. I think you'll enjoy the quaint little children at least as much as I do. I arranged the pictures myself for the most part. The day before yesterday I went on a beautiful cycling tour with Pastor Schminke to his village of Rockensüss. I rode back alone by night along a beautiful stretch that wove downward from the heights through deep woods. We had a very good bible class while there with some friendly farmers, and I intend to return. On the 30th I'm going to hold two sermons and two meetings in his village. Pray about this.

Now, God protect you. May he give you joy upon joy and power upon power.

Yours confidently and firmly in Jesus,
Eberhard

Langeoog
August 24, 1908

My only beloved Ebbo,

I just now received your two loving letters and am sitting down right away to answer them. I'm *very* sorry I told Clara so much. We were having such a good time sharing together, and then I told her something about the difficulties you were experiencing. It didn't cross my mind that you didn't want me to. That's no excuse, of course, but I want you to know how it happened. What's more – and this is very unpleasant for me to have to admit to you – I probably did tell Clara about the Frankes' behavior, though I didn't tell her the most unbelievable part. As far as von Gerdtell is concerned, I think I only said that you had some problem with him. I told her we thought it was because you and I hadn't become Baptists. But I think I also said the matter was already being resolved, and that you had said it was grace from the Lord that you hadn't become dependent on von Gerdtell. I didn't say anything specific about what he said or wrote. I'm sure that's everything. I could, of course, tell you everything better in person. I hope this won't cause too much damage. It would be terrible if you feel you can't be open with me – though if that's the case, then it's better that you aren't. I just can't seem to keep quiet, however much I want to.

I'm very glad, though, that von Gerdtell has seen the light. Let's not hold anything against him anymore. You can tell him that from me, too. After all, he was led on to it, and we even know where his suspicions came from. My Ebbo, we're so happy in the Lord and in each other that maybe we don't need any other people. If God sends us something like this, perhaps he does it to teach us not to be oversensitive. I'm still too touchy on occasion, but then I remember that this is a sin, and the feeling goes away. I'm also glad that the two of you can work together again. Just don't get involved in anything that could hamper you in any way!

I don't have a beach chair yet. My cold is too bad now to be able to sit on the beach. I will go to the doctor here tomorrow unless it gets better. I don't believe I'll be able to stay until September 12; I'm thinking of leaving on the 5th. If only my cold would go away! But I want to get this letter off. Please forgive me for everything. I'll write to Clara tomorrow.

In him,
your bride

In late August, Eberhard's intention to be baptized and leave the state church became public knowledge, casting into doubt his chances at sitting for a doctoral examination in theology. Both he and Emmy had prepared themselves for this, but still, the prospect of having to begin a whole new course of study (he eventually chose philosophy) was daunting.

Bebra
August 28, 1908

John 10:28: "I give them eternal life, and they shall never perish; no one can snatch them out of my hand."

My dearest bride,

What's going to happen to us? What will the coming winter and summer bring? We don't know, but we can be blissfully certain that Jesus cares for us and that we'll never be lost! Most probably we'll go through many troubles and difficulties, especially with our beloved parents, in regard to our engagement. But let's arm ourselves for this and take up the right stance from the very start. Our only resolve must be to live undividedly for God and, in so living, to be as deep a blessing and strengthening as possible to each other.

Let us completely free ourselves from all other wishes, even if we bring them before God. It's in this sense that I am directing my determined prayers that we might marry in the year 1909, so that we can be a greater blessing and joy to each other and to many others. How he decides to lead us doesn't worry me. I'm certain he'll do everything in the best way. Perhaps it will be very different from what we expect or request, but still the best and most glorious way. I'm sure you will also want to unite with me in this trust! May my time in Halle help save many students and others, and may many believers be led to surrender their lives fully to Jesus!

The latest news from Pastor Hänisch is very significant. According to it, I'll probably (in fact almost certainly) *not* be allowed to sit for the exam. Further, it's quite likely I'll be asked to come to Breslau in the next few weeks by General Superintendent Nottebohm. I only hope Papa won't reproach me regarding this state of affairs. How can he? What do you think? I've done my duty to the fullest, sent in long, written reports, and acted with sincerity. If I'm rejected now, I can't be blamed for that.

I sorely missed, in today's sweet letter, a detailed response to my correspondence with Hänisch. When I'm taking such enormously momentous steps, it's infinitely important to me to know your precise judgment and impressions. If by chance you haven't made sense of all the mass of material I sent, I'll gladly send it to you again, along with my parents' letters. Whatever the case may be, I need you at my side, in your thoughts and with your discernment, and I covet your help to attain and maintain the clearest stand possible in everything I do.

As regards von Gerdtell, I'm sure you promised me not to say anything about him. It's especially painful that you did, now that he's being so friendly, but let's not write about this anymore, and just do better in the future. He's been nicer and more trusting than ever, and takes the blame for what happened on himself again and again. He's done an enormous amount for me, really everything he possibly could. It's a pity that he hardly knows you at all yet. He sends you his warmest greetings. Everything's completely clear between him and me now, thank God, but I'm still going to be cautious, so that no new misunderstandings arise, and I am going to work entirely independently from him. May God be with you, my dearest bride, and strengthen you.

In Jesus, your faithful Ebbo

Langeoog
August 31, 1908

1 John 4:19: "We love because he first loved us."

My Ebbo,

Before the mail leaves today, I wanted to tell you that I thought of leaving on Friday. The ferries that leave the following days aren't suitable, so that would make my stay a whole week longer, and everything is so expensive. As for how I get home, I thought of staying about a week in Salzwedel, and then another week each in Stappenbeck and Mühlingen, so that I'd be home in three weeks.

I'm actually rather frightened about going home, you know. Papa will probably kick up a tremendous row about your being barred from taking your exam. But I've had such a beautiful, quiet time that I should have strength for struggles now. If only the Lord would show me a place to go for the coming winter. I'd really like to get a job nursing again, but I don't know whether I can because of my health.

The reason I didn't write more in response to Pastor Hänisch's correspondence is that I don't really understand the whole thing very well. Why did you add that to your application, and why didn't you inquire last year whether you'd be allowed to take the exam, if you intended then to have yourself baptized? It seems that with the situation as it is now, taking your exam won't even come into question. Until now I thought it was impossible only if you'd already been baptized. I wanted to ask you about it in person, since I couldn't make sense of what Clara said. You sent me tons of material, but then you wanted to have it all back again right away. That's why I don't really have a clear picture of the matter. All the same, I trust you not to act in an ill-considered way.

In regard to your parents' letters about all this, I'm sure they mean to be loving, but they don't understand us. I think my parents will be *much* angrier than yours. Fortunately we don't need to be held back by either family. I'm praying for your trip to Breslau.

Meanwhile I'm grateful to be getting acquainted with so many people here. Yesterday I went to church with Fräulein Freyberger and Fräulein Kraedtke. The pastor preached on Luke 7:41–43 and spoke pretty plainly. In the afternoon Fräulein Bertram asked me to read a very boring scientific lecture with her. We went into the dunes to do this and afterward got into an earnest talk about the sin of men and our own sin. Fräulein Bertram asked me whether I looked down on people who aren't believers. I had to laugh about that! How can I, who have been saved myself, look down on anyone for whom Christ died? I told her that I could only feel sorry for them. I also gave her the red book by von Gerdtell about the atonement of Christ, and have great hopes that it will help her. But now I must close, my Ebbo. Please greet the Wiegands.

Commending you to the Lord in constant love,

your bride

Bebra
August 31, 1908

My beloved bride,

Yesterday in Rockensüss I was deeply and powerfully blessed through four sermons and talks I gave. I'm sure God blessed it for my listeners, too, including Georg Herde, with whom I had a very special time of fellowship. He didn't leave until noon today. My texts were 1 Timothy 1:12–15 and 1 John 2:12–14. Even greater, however, is the blessing I've received from reading Dr. Pierson's biography of George Müller: a glorious, deep book that Viebahn recommended and which Gotthelf gave me as a gift. Never in my life has praying in faith become so real to me as through this book. Faith in praying has always been one of the most essential elements of my relationship to Jesus; but until now, I haven't taken my stand on faith alone, on simple prayer, on *nothing but God* for my outward life and its requirements. It's been clear to me for a long time, though, that God wants me to live *from faith alone,* so that his victories might be shown in my life as well. So from now on I'm more determined than ever to take this stand.

One of the most significant experiences I've had of praying with a firm, sure faith in being answered (and therefore with the certainty of attaining victory, whatever the circumstances), was our engagement. March 29, 1907, was one of the most important milestones in my inner life, quite apart from the fact that it was the second most blissful day of my life.

And just as we entered our lifelong bond, which will last into eternity, with such an amazing experience of faith, so let us continue it with due steadfastness. I think the Lord is trying to speak to us by bringing us to the point where, in all areas of our life, we must rely on him alone, in the prayer of faith (and thus in the advance assurance of victory). This is how I want to approach the public announcement of our engagement, the question of our future income, and everything else we need. Let's keep living this way, and so become surer in our faith. No human being, not even the most powerful and important, can withstand what God wills. So let us remain one in him and keep quietly praying to him with full trust in his leading (not in our own) until he answers us. Let's do the same as regards my employment in Halle, my exams, and everything.

And let's deal in the same way with our sins and weaknesses. I have much worse and bigger ones than you, but it's vital that God grants you the grace to be able to keep quiet about things where necessary, and yet remain happy and innocent. I'd venture to say that the largest part of what a man truly experiences of God must be kept quiet if his honor and the trust of men are not to be broken, or the cause damaged. (That means, my dearest, that you should have asked me before writing to Else about my difficulties in regard to the exam. I might have allowed it with certain conditions, but in this case I *had* written and asked you to say nothing.) O Emmy, we need to pray that we stand completely before God. Then everyone will see that even amid the greatest sufferings and hardest disappointments we are happy in Jesus, people who should be envied, not pitied, *because they trust God completely.*

Now, sweetheart, I want to thank you very warmly for your latest letters, though I'm not in agreement with your travel plans. First of all, it was stupid to tie yourself to a return ticket, since it isn't one bit cheaper. Second, I can't understand why you want to leave already now. I beg you with my whole heart: stay on Langeoog until September 11 or 12 and don't arrive back in Halle before the end of September! Still better, come only at the beginning of October. I ask this out of sheer love and by no means want to try to coerce you.

Regarding my application, I'm certain that I acted rightly. As long as I would have kept secret my intention to be baptized, there would not (of course) have been any obstacle to my taking the exam. But I would have been a hypocrite, deceiver, and swindler if I'd sat for it without making my plans known, and then immediately skipped out. And that's also the way others would have seen it. As for my detractors, they would have exploited it. That's what Hänisch thinks, too. He felt it was absolutely necessary for me to make this point clear, in fact he thinks the most correct route would be for me to forgo the exam entirely.

It's terribly important, dear Emmy, that you have a thorough understanding of my decision. I know we couldn't consider it together beforehand, on account of the great distance between us and the short time, but I'm sending you the entire story once again, and I'd like to ask you to study it very carefully. Grasp the main points, and don't send it back until you're completely clear about it. (It's obvious that Papa and Clara's understanding of it is untenable, because it's not really an honest appraisal.)

In my opinion it's still up in the air whether I'll be admitted or not. But the Lord will decide, and we must trust him firmly and joyfully. Earlier I thought that only the completed step of baptism (and not the mere intention) would bar me from sitting for the exam, and that *is* the information Papa gave me at the time – at least that's how I understood it. In any case, the final decision is in the hands of the Breslau Consistory alone, though they may ask the High Consistory for advice. In short, it's very unclear which way the decision will go. Because of this I feel it would be wrong to inform our parents and brothers and sisters of anything beforehand (except possibly Else, as one who will pray about it), but if I travel via Halle, I might have to give some hint.

Well, my darling, I must close since you have to get this letter and everything tomorrow, if at all possible. Pray hard for me that in this time of decision I remain completely holy before him, full of his spirit, constantly prayerful, and ultimately a complete man of God!

In great love and trusting our faithful, strong Lord completely for you and for myself,

your bridegroom

While Eberhard traveled to Breslau, where he learned that the university would bar him from taking his examination, Emmy returned to Halle. Traveling via Salzwedel, she visited the hospital where she had worked earlier, and found it understaffed. The head deaconess tried to persuade her to stay and work, even if only temporarily, and she promised to think about it. Though not fully recovered from her recent illness, she was looking for a place to live and work away from her family, and this one seemed ideal.

Breslau
September 21, 1908

John 16:23: "I tell you the truth, my Father will give you whatever you ask in my name."

Most beloved Emmy,

Already yesterday when I saw your letter to Mama, but still more today when your sweet letter to me arrived, I had to fight very hard against excitement, worry, and anger. But after spending about an hour by the Oder River reading John 14, I can now write to you without any resentment, though still with a little disappointment and worry.

My dearest little dear! Did you not receive the telegram I sent, indicating that I found your travel plans distressing? I sent it because I didn't know how else to get a letter to you. And how did your parents take the news about my exam? It's terribly sad that you're home just at this point, when your presence can only make things worse, *and* after I asked you not to. You can't go back to working in Salzwedel! That you gave in to pressure there shows a lack of firm character. I perceive in it a desire to please people and a certain cowardice that tries to avoid a momentarily embarrassing situation, instead of remaining courageously on the path of duty. *Please* be more prudent in the future in such enormously important matters, and keep in close touch with me. Don't you realize that your parents' attitude to our engagement and wedding, and your reception at home, may all be endangered by this foolish haste?

Fortunately, the Lord cares for us and allows our stupidities to serve for the best. How I would have liked to talk the doctors' questions over with you before each step! Dr. Witthauer's opinion is by no means sufficient for me. At the most, he can support your refusal to return to Salzwedel. Well, my much-too-good-natured darling, I submit to the situation as it is, however untenable it may be, and to Jesus. You can be sure, my dearest, that our time together will be happy and victorious and that I love you every bit as much as if you'd acted entirely in accordance with my wishes.

I really love the photos from Hamburg. You look so delightful and joyous, especially on the one with Hermann. May God protect you and keep you firm and cheerful.

Praying for you constantly and completely yours in Jesus,
your loyal Ebbo

Halle
September 24, 1908

My beloved,

I received your letter this morning. I'm glad you aren't upset with me anymore. But you know, my darling, I feel as if you're always forbidding me from doing this or that, and I'm often in a real bind about what to do when I can't immediately ask you for advice. Of course you have the right to do this, but I believe I've mostly acted as you'd want me to, even if it looked like disobedience at first glance. And you get so angry so quickly and let it out when others are around! I'm only trying to do what's right.

Leaving that, I agree that you shouldn't tell my parents anything until we ourselves can talk and are clear about God's will for us. It would be very good if we met again some time soon, but maybe it would work better at a friend's house rather than somewhere outdoors. I won't tell my parents anything about your coming to Halle until we can approach them with a full-fledged plan. We can't possibly comply with *their ideas* with regard to our future.

Today there was another big drama at home. Monika thinks I expressed my opinion too innocently again. But I don't even really know what it's all about. Last night Else and I went to a wonderful bible class held by von der Recke at the Martinis'. It was a farewell class for him. Can you believe that the police have ordered him out of the city limits for having dared, as a Russian subject, to draw souls away from the established church? In specific, he held large baptisms here three times. He *has* to leave by tonight, or he'll be arrested. Isn't that incredible? Pastor Hobbing also put a warning in the church bulletin, claiming that von der Recke was trying to found a "baptismal sect" in Halle.

We're in such a terrible situation here at home, too. Offensive remarks are forever being made about us, and my parents are constantly suspicious of Else and me. They keep trying to distance Monika from us and are always warning her about us. The way they act is simply horrible. Mama recently said that though she loved us as her children, she felt completely separated from us otherwise. She then said to Monika, "Are you with us and Pastor Hobbing, or with Emmy and Else?" Good old Monika replied, "Emmy and Else," so of course there was a new scene.

I should close, though, so that you can get this letter tomorrow. God protect you, my dearest. I'm also looking forward so much to seeing you. Let's be faithful in everything and do his will alone.

In love, your faithful Emmy

Breslau
September 25, 1908

Follow Jesus onward!

My only sweetheart,

First let me tell you, my darling, that I will examine myself closely in the future before forbidding you to do anything, and will do better from now on. Believe me, my love, your independence is very important to me, and it's only right that you always do what seems right before God. I have full trust in your decisions, and I know they often agree with my intentions, even though outwardly they may seem to go against my previously expressed wishes. Should you, my heart, be quite certain before God that Jesus wants something that I don't want, then you should *always* act, even if in contradiction to my will. It's just that in certain areas – particularly that of your health and your timidity, which at times don't allow you to take a firm enough stand – I believe you could use support in carrying out the will of God which is already clear to you. I'll always be glad to give you that support by clearly expressing my own will. Certainly I find it upsetting when I sense that you're acting against my will to your own detriment. But, beloved Emmy, I desire *more than ever* to keep a check on myself so that Jesus can overcome all the faults of my temperament. Above all, I no longer want to reproach you, nor will I express definite wishes beforehand either, until I've learned and understood the situation from your perspective. Nor will I, under any circumstances, ever again mention anything about you that I don't agree with in the presence of others. Please forgive me, dear heart, for having done that at times. I will not do it again, with the sole exception of instances in which Jesus' honor and truth demand it. Please accept my promise that from today on I want to be more loving, more tender, more patient, and more tactful in all things. Forgive my crudeness, and trust that the Lord will make my character both firm *and* considerate, manly *and* tender.

Emmy! How happy I am that I'll be able to kiss you again so soon! Then you will know without a doubt how *terribly* much I love you and how *dreadfully* sorry I am that I have hurt you. You are my life in Jesus, and without full harmony and unity with you I cannot exist. We're fully one now, though, aren't we, my heart?

As regards the question of how to approach my exam with Papa, I'm at a complete loss. We'll need to talk it over thoroughly before we can come to any truly clear or conclusive decision. I understand your suggestion of meeting at a friend's house; however, I think it would be better if we met at the Hunter's Garden. We can't be reproached for meeting there if we're found out later. I suggest we meet there on Friday, October 2. I'll wait for you from 2:45 on. Come by way of the churchyard. After that I'll travel on to Leipzig, Dresden, and Berlin (also Freienwalde), and get back to Halle around the 16th. That time we can meet at a friend's house, and in the evening I'll show up at your parents'. I won't mention the time of my arrival. In this way we'll gain two weeks to think things over quietly before God. What do you say to this? Should you in any way be against it, I could, of course, travel directly into Halle on the 2nd, although it seems more risky.

God protect you, my Emmy! Let's not allow anything to confuse us but continue to believe in God, firmly and joyfully.

Your Ebbo

I'm very sorry that von der Recke has had to leave Halle. I'd have liked to get to know him. However, I think that what he's gone through for Jesus' sake is wonderful and glorious.

In October, Eberhard returned to Halle to start his new doctoral program in philosophy and to continue serving the city's "newly awakened." He and Emmy met immediately, first privately and then at the von Hollander house. It wasn't long before a heated argument erupted over the cancelled theology examination. Heinrich von Hollander accused Eberhard of breaking his trust and of "licentiousness and a lack of chivalry," and declared that he was morally unreliable. Eberhard demanded that he take back these insults and clear his honor in the eyes of his bride-to-be, and then stormed out of the house. When Emmy protested to her parents, they informed her that she was no longer welcome under their roof.

After this falling-out, Emmy's health deteriorated. Eberhard found her a place in the household of a certain Pastor Köhler in Berlin, where she cared for the family's children part of the day, but was able to spend most of her time resting and recuperating. Pastor Köhler had left the state church for reasons of conscience and was closely linked with the revival movement. Emmy enjoyed her work tremendously and also the chance the Pastor gave her to invite young women to a weekly tea, at which she led discussions on inner questions and sought to "guide those enslaved by sin to find freedom in Jesus."

With the uncertainties over his exam finally clear, Eberhard felt it was time to have himself baptized. This long-anticipated event took place quietly, probably on October 25. As reported beforehand to Emmy, he purchased "a nice white flannel suit" for the occasion and promised her that, "if the same material can be used for women, I'll get you some so that you can make yourself a nice dress in which you can be baptized at Christmas." Although barred from visiting the von Hollander house, he nevertheless met as often as he could with Else and Monika.

Meanwhile his parents, beside themselves with fury, sent him a letter disowning him and banishing him from their house. It was a heavy blow, though not surprising, given his father's position as a professor of theology. Dr. Carl Franklin Arnold, stolid churchman that he was, was deeply humiliated to have a son who publicly undermined everything he taught in the lecture hall. Elisabeth

Arnold accused her wayward child of "foolish, shortsighted views" and "loveless inconsideration," and prophesied, "If you do not return to sobriety, your future will be dark and the rest of your life unhappy."

Having been cut off by their families on both sides, Eberhard and Emmy were now free, at long last, to make their engagement public after a strenuous year and a half of secrecy. In order to make good on his agreement with Emmy's father, however, Eberhard still had to pass his doctoral examination – now in philosophy – before the wedding.

Financially, they were now on their own. Eberhard had a small inheritance from one of his aunts, and Emmy had access to a modest family endowment, as well as legacies earmarked to furnish their future home. But apart from this they were forced to depend on others – and on Providence – for their daily existence.

Misunderstandings

Unwelcome at either of their homes, Eberhard and Emmy spent Christmas together in Berlin, where Emmy was baptized on December 22, 1908. In January, Eberhard returned to his studies and his work in the revival movement in Halle.

Halle
January 27, 1909

Most beloved Emmy,

The last days have been so full that I'm only now managing to tell you of the many things I've experienced. But your letters have been a great refreshment and strengthening to me through the grind.

Since I've again and again missed a truly deep response to the commands and thoughts of God among SCM members here, a recent encounter I had with the power of a genuine awakening was all the more shaking. It took place in Caesar, a high school student who had attended some of my meetings in Erfurt. After entrenching himself in an atheistic worldview, he suddenly came out with all sorts of horrible sins and revealed the main obstacle to his finding new life: he feared the serious consequences of conversion. That's when the real struggle began. Again and again he sought cover in atheistic doubts: "What would happen if Christ weren't living after all, and I find that I've placed myself on the side of someone who doesn't even exist?" etc. I pointed out to him the awful cunning and power of Satan in binding him through servitude to sin and the most incredible delusions. Further, I showed him the grace that was drawing him toward Jesus and God, and how he was sinning against it. At last, after two hours of struggle, he broke down so dreadfully, in such an excited, shattered state, that he couldn't stand upright but fell to the floor. Convulsively jerking, he clenched his fists and affirmed over and over, while sobbing, "I *want* it, I *want* to be converted! Oh, if only he could accept me!" It was difficult for me to set him upright and point him to Jesus. Only after I could turn him from his dreadful agitation toward Jesus and to a clear, deliberate decision of faith (I used many helpful words from the Bible) could he get hold of himself and assure me that he now had faith. I also told him that the devil would probably afflict him again with the discouragement and emotional reactions that *always* follow such agitation. On Monday evening he told me how he'd gone home rejoicing after this experience, confessed Jesus, and witnessed to an unbelieving cousin. He had been extremely happy. But not much later he was unhappier than ever, just as I predicted. So I directed him away from feelings and toward the Lord, and he said he did want to remain faithful. He also begged me very earnestly for intercession. We really must pray for him, because he's a weak character, having been in such bondage until now.

Because of this talk, which I couldn't possibly break off, I arrived somewhat late at the class for the newly converted, where there were about twenty-six people. We're now going to move the class to the Passage Hall, and hope for further growth that way. This time we spoke about our attitude to the world (according to 1 John 2). I also spoke openly about the theater and dancing, and this was well received. Following the class, I answered questions from four of the newly converted people. One of these had been invited to a big party which was to conclude with a ball, lasting until four in the morning, and sought my advice. Another had been forbidden by her parents to attend the "baptistic" Sunday school. The third was being harassed by her husband and felt tempted to go into the world. She wrote me a long letter about this, and we talked until quite late yesterday. The fourth was Caesar, who needed encouraging again. With one of the above-mentioned I was also led to speak about baptism, which she didn't seem to understand yet, however. In the evening I was asked about my attitude to the church, to the Lord's Supper, and baptism, but I found little receptivity when I witnessed. The good ladies I spoke to were more interested in the beauty of the church building and the tone of the organ. I sincerely hope that complete biblical truth will penetrate.

On Monday morning I had a difficult private talk with a mentally ill business man who has ruined himself terribly by sin, and even now talks about his dark past and present in a matter-of-fact way inconceivable to me. I reproached him energetically and held out to him the saving grace of Jesus. He promised me "to concern himself with it" and came to the evening lecture, but so far he has not shown any signs of a conversion.

At 3:30 in the afternoon another student came whom the Lord has evidently blessed greatly. Over the past week he's visited a high school senior by the name of Luckow (who was awakened through von Gerdtell), has spoken with Caesar a lot, and confronted them both rather sharply, telling them that the issue is really whether they *want* conversion or not. Apparently another bible class pupil challenged his mother to decide completely for Christ, and also approached two of his classmates, hoping to bring them to conversion. It's really wonderful when Christ leads people so radically and completely to such a decision and to his power. And these incidents show what this depends on: the honesty of the will.

At the evening meeting, which was well attended, I spoke about Old Testament law and about the gospel, obedience, and faith. I felt imperfect and weak, but on the other hand some of my listeners said it had been the best lecture I'd given. Four people were converted (stood up, expressed themselves, and prayed), among them the husband of Frau Mensel, who had been converted in the previous meeting. Until the meeting he had subscribed to the philosophy of Kant and Schopenhauer and claimed he just was not able to believe. Oddly, I had just spoken about the weakness of Kant's categorical imperative, though I had no idea about Herr Mensel.

Caesar accompanied me most of the way home and seems to be firm and decisive. At the house where I've been staying,

I unfortunately found a Baptist brother in my room, who had come from out of town to my lecture. He questioned me until about two o'clock in the morning or later about all sorts of difficult issues. Added to this was my discomfort in sleeping with a strange person in the same room. Next time I'll move into a hotel.

At 8:30 in the morning on Tuesday, I had to rush to a personal talk with the newly converted Wiskemanns, whose landlord had poured out his heart to me in a letter nearly as thick as a book. They're wonderful new converts, but unfortunately are mired in business problems. He accompanied me to the train. Hardly had I been able to take a short breather in Halle when one visitor and then another and another came without interruption. I wasn't alone until after twelve o'clock. On top of this, something I said about a lack of inner zeal in the SCM met with agitation and strong protest. I'm actually thankful for this, however, since something is at last *moving,* at a time when our bible classes keep getting smaller and smaller. (In 1906–07, sixty to eighty people would come on a Thursday. Now it's fourteen or fifteen!)

Today was about the same. From two o'clock until now (it's already 11:30), people have been coming without interruption to talk. As a result, I'll have to bring this letter to the station as soon as I finish it, and won't be able to answer all the important things in *yours* until tomorrow. Pray that I keep finding more peace and strength for my studies. I just can't go on, the way these days have been.

In deepest love,
your faithful Ebbo

While Emmy was in Berlin looking after Pastor Köhler's children, Frau Köhler traveled to Halle and dropped in on the von Hollander parents. Later she met Eberhard, too, and he pressed a gift for Emmy into her hands.

Berlin
January 30, 1909

My deeply beloved Ebbo,

You're really too much, sending me such delightful things again through Frau Köhler. That charming little basket with violets, and the fine fruits! You're much too good!

By the way, Frau Köhler told me all about you – that you are very nice and that we should marry soon. But she was shocked by how Mama treats me. I myself am really angry with my mother. What is she thinking? Papa is a whole different story. He actually acts like a father to me. I feel sorry for him, but I can always find a way to get along with him. But what should I do about Mama? The way she behaves is impossible! Frau Köhler says she wants to write to her about it. *That* will be something. But I doubt you'll be able to visit them. *They* offended you – *you* didn't offend them. Why don't you let them take the first step? In any case, I don't know what you would say if you met with them. Well, we must let ourselves be led by the Lord. If he shows us a way, we'll follow.

I was very disappointed that Else wasn't allowed to come with Frau Köhler. I don't understand why she didn't warn me beforehand, instead of letting me get my hopes up. Please ask her or Olga and Monika about it. Yesterday we had a good bible class again, with nine young girls. Clara also attended. We're working through the story of Elijah now, as an example of a man who lived undividedly for God. Yesterday we read through 1 Kings 17. Clara wants to come again. She, too, was disappointed that Else didn't come. Today I have the bible circle for children in the afternoon, and Dora's coming to see me in the evening.

I'm looking forward very eagerly to your arrival, my love. It makes me so happy every time I think about Christmas. I'm also so happy about your work in Erfurt. God protect you on your journey there tomorrow.

Your loving, faithful bride

At the end of March 1909, Eberhard moved to Erlangen to complete the last phase of his studies. In the meantime, Emmy's parents finally allowed her to return home to Halle. She found the atmosphere there unbearably tense, though, and was glad when news of yet another employment opportunity came her way: a group of young children with whooping cough had been sequestered at a saline spa in Kösen and needed a nurse to look after them. Eberhard, however, worried that the job would be too strenuous for her. He was also rankled by the von Hollanders' apparent lack of concern for their daughter's health, and decided to ask them instead to pay their daughter's way to Bebra, where she could relax and recuperate with the Wiegands. Emmy wrote warning him that this request would only heighten tensions at home, especially with her mother, and begged him not to get involved.

Erlangen
April 5, 1909

Psalm 22:26: "The poor will eat and be satisfied; they who seek the Lord will praise him – may your hearts live forever!"

My dear, sweet Emmy,

Of course I'm not at all angry, my darling, and I'm not sad anymore either, though I don't think your point of view is the right one in this case. What I'm sad about is our separation, and it wouldn't be honest to say that I've been victorious. But I will trust and conquer. Psalm 22:4–5: "In you our fathers put their trust; they trusted and you delivered them. They cried to you and were saved; in you they trusted and were not disappointed."

Regarding the enclosed letter to your parents, isn't it quite harmless? Please send it back to me by return mail, and then I'll send it to them. Trust me, everything will work out just fine, and you'll be happy about the outcome. By the way, I want to let you in on a secret plan of mine: I want to spend a Sunday early in May with you in Jena (or Weimar or that general area). For this to happen, you'd have to leave the day after Mama's birthday so as to be free on the 1st (or better, the 7th) of May. Keep this secret – no one but the two of us should know about it.

With ardent, constant love,
your Ebbo

Halle
April 6, 1909

Dearest Ebbo,

My deep thanks for your letter. How I look forward to the 1st of May! That would be so special if we could be together for a day! I'm looking forward to it very much. But darling, *please don't send that letter.* It will be no help at all. We won't get anywhere with it, other than receiving unpleasant remarks about being too demanding. Please believe me. Else and Monika can't do anything either. As it is, Mama rebukes me because Papa and Olga "never travel," though Papa himself would gladly give me travel money and is very unhappy about Mama's stance.

In deep love, and looking forward tremendously to seeing you again,

your faithful Emmy

Erlangen
April 7, 1909

Beloved Emmy,

It wasn't right that you didn't return the letter to me!

1) The letter to Mama is my duty, even if it's of no use.

2) The 100 Marks from Riga are *only* for outfitting you when we get married and must not be used in any other way.

3) Money is not the point. We will always have money.

4) Please travel to Kösen between the 14th and 17th (the 18th at the latest). From there, you could travel on for several weeks to Bebra, and possibly Seligenthal.

5) Saturday, May 6, we'll meet in Weimar, God willing, or wherever you wish (Kösen, Jena, Naumburg?).

6) By the way, you cannot give the photos of us to Papa or Mama (nor to our siblings) until Papa's reproaches and accusations have been cleared up. I'm glad he's friendlier and have great hopes.

God protect you. Loving you endlessly,
your Ebbo

My studies are going along fine, but my frame of mind and attempts to be purified are *not.* Pray very hard! May Jesus and God help me.

Erlangen
April 10, 1909

Dear, sweet Emmy,

I'm glad you aren't angry with me, but hope you'll understand me more quickly in such matters. I'm also very happy about the things you received, and that Mama is somewhat friendlier to you. I will, however, be much more at ease once you've left Halle; I hope you won't need to stay there all summer. It always makes me uneasy to think of your being there. Of course you're quite right, my darling: you know the circumstances at home better than I. But you mustn't overlook the fact that I'm always letting myself be swayed by your soothing advice, as I was in this case too. The letter to Mama would most likely have turned out differently if you hadn't put the brakes on me as you did. Still, I'm terribly happy that I have you, the very dearest of all girls. I'm finding out why the Lord made husband *and* wife, and feel I'm learning all the time from your prized womanliness.

However, that just strengthens (rather than hinders) me in my conviction that I've listened to you and your sisters too much in family matters. I believe I can get furthest and attain the most by masculine straightforwardness. I also feel that representing *my own* character and allowing it to operate naturally is the only way that my witness for Jesus can be powerful and victorious.

But I must close. I'm terrifically happy about the doctor's opinion! What kindness from the Lord! Now Emmy, please write and tell me immediately:

1) exactly when you will leave
2) how you plan to arrange the journey
3) whether we can spend May 8 together in Weimar
4) how Mama received my letter.

Pray for me always, and always love me.

Living solely for you, in Jesus,
your Eberhard

Halle
April 11, 1909

My dearest Ebbo,

My heartfelt thanks for your letter. I'm so glad that nothing can come between us, because I love you *tremendously*, even if you don't always comply with my will. I also realize that you're right in wanting to educate me in that. But you must comply with it to some extent, don't you think?

Please allow me to give my parents a picture. They'll be very offended if I don't, and they keep asking me for one. Today during the Lord's Supper the matter with Lucia Franke came to my mind in such a way that I let the cup pass by me. God protect you!

With deepest love and kisses,
your loyal Emmy

Erlangen
April 11, 1909

My Emmy,

I really wish I could write you a happy letter, because my sole concern is that you're completely happy and love me fully! But I'm tormented by what's maybe a totally unnecessary worry, and the only way to get rid of it is to write all about it to you.

I'm sure you know how very happy it makes me when your family, and Papa in particular, are friendly to you and don't cause scenes, and my joy would be boundless if nothing more stood between Papa and us, and he was converted. That isn't the case yet, however. I love Papa dearly and pray often and earnestly for him. I especially keep a framed picture of him in front of me because of this. But, dear Emmy, the fact remains unchanged that until now Papa has treated me like an unreliable and morally doubtful person, and has continually reproached me with suggestions of dishonesty and rascality. As long as this state of affairs is not fully resolved by a clear assurance to the contrary from his side, I will by no means give the impression that all is in order between us. Above all, I will not present my picture to someone who has assessed and designated me in such a negative manner. That is why I remain dead set against our picture being given to your parents.

I believe this might be the best occasion for you, my dear bride, to have a quiet and serious talk with Papa, where you can tell him that until he plainly declares his full trust in my character (as regards both the past and the future), something will stand between us and therefore between you and him.

My worry, beloved Emmy – please forgive me for saying this – is that you in your gentle way have allowed yourself to be won over by Papa's friendliness. We must be grateful for it, but it is certainly not sufficient. Because of your attitude to him, he might think that there is nothing between us.

I believe that you're the only person capable of clarifying all this for Papa, as long as you find strength from the Lord to combine love and wisdom with unyielding determination and transparency. It would be awful for me, and worse than anything up to this point, if your parents got the impression that you've changed your mind regarding me, and that I can be isolated (like a problem) and simply passed over as "stubborn and rude." If your parents continue to relate to you in this way, they will naturally be indifferent to my thoughts and feelings. That's why I sometimes fear we've gone too far with you staying at home so long. The only way forward is for you to tell Papa that we have wanted to show him our love, but are unable to have community with him as long as there is disharmony and divisiveness in the family. Above all, however, let's pray unceasingly for his conversion. I love and honor him as much as hardly anyone else besides you, especially because he loves you so much.

Now, God protect you. I've worked all morning so am now going to take a bicycle ride into the mountains.

Thanks for your Easter letter, by the way. I love you unutterably and ask for your love in return.

Your faithful Ebbo

Halle
April 12, 1909

My best beloved Ebbo,

You really don't need to worry. How could you ever think that I don't represent you loyally enough! I really love you alone and need no one else but you. It cuts me to the heart whenever I remember how shockingly Papa treated you last fall (and me as well). I simply can't understand that you think I want to forget about that without clearing it up. I've made my stand clear by not letting my parents persuade me to stay home this summer, which is what they want. And if you feel so strongly about it, I won't even think of giving them a picture. I can only tell you, dear Ebbo, that I've never loved you so much as I do now and am extremely sad that you would question my love. I'll speak with Papa right away, my darling, so that there's no misunderstanding. And tomorrow I'm buying flowers for Mama from you.

About our trip: I have to see the doctor again on Wednesday morning about my nose, etc. He's still doing injections. He also believes a change of air is the best thing. I must close and go out, my love. The doctor wants me to spend as much time as possible outdoors.

Loving you boundlessly in him,
your faithful Emmy

In Eberhard's next letter he assured Emmy of his confidence in her, and asked forgiveness for hurting her with his questions. "I only worried that you, like so many women and girls, might easily lose sight of the situation at hand, which is basically unchanged, even though Papa has suddenly become so loving and friendly in every way." On April 15, Emmy left for Kösen. Eberhard intensified his studies as he strove to prepare himself for his final examinations, which were now rescheduled for the end of 1909.

Erlangen
April 21, 1909

Most beloved bride,

You'll hardly be able to imagine how much I'm accomplishing each day through the Lord's strength and grace:

1) Forty-five to fifty pages of Kant. This is definitely the most difficult philosophical material. Von Gerdtell claims it's completely incomprehensible, but I don't agree with him since I've already worked through, understood, and learned one of his works, and a solid portion of a second one. This is the most important part of my studies.

2) Seventeen to twenty pages of Greek philosophy by Zeller. Selecting the most important sections is holding me up quite a bit.

3) About fifteen pages of transcendental philosophy by Professor Rickert. Compared to Kant, this is child's play.

4) Now and then some Nietzsche. I'm completely done with two significant books now, and hope to get to the end of

three more by May 8. My only worry is that the interruption caused by giving lectures (from the 28th on) will take at least two to three hours of my time every day, and even now I'm having to utilize every minute to manage the assignments in front of me.

You can hardly believe how thankful I am to our Lord for this, since I see his blessing in it and know that it is he alone who grants success.

I feel completely carried by your prayers in this and am infinitely thankful that the Lord is conquering and calming more and more my immeasurably strong passions of longing for you. You will only understand how infinitely much your indescribably sweet letters mean to me if you are able to imagine my longing for you, the intensity of my studies, and my utter loneliness here. Oh, how I praise the Lord that I have you and that if his grace continues to shine so wondrously on us, I might be allowed to have you completely as my own, in the eyes of the world as well, before this year is over!

Yes, we have a great deal to recount and tell each other. I have lots to tell, my sweet little bird, and am eager to hear all that *you* have to tell me. Write down everything you want to talk about. Since you intend to travel on Friday, I'll send my next letter to Bebra. Please keep writing to me often! I could still say and thank and ask and tell you lots, but I must close. And I'll be writing less and less as time goes on, since in great hope for our happy future, I'll be working harder and harder to meet my glorious goal.

Your Ebbo

Bebra
April 30, 1909

My most deeply beloved Ebbo,

Warmest thanks for your letter! It brought me deep joy. But don't overstrain yourself. Whether you get your doctor's degree half a year later than you hoped won't make such a big difference in the end. But if your nerves are run down, what will we do then? Please, please be sensible. Please think of the future! Don't damage yourself permanently with strain. I pray constantly for your health, but you must also do your part, or I'll be worried all the time and won't be well either.

And please also pray hard that I become completely free from all sin, so that I can walk more closely with Jesus. I wish the same for you.

I was just thinking, my Ebbo, that when we were talking about the wedding, you may have completely misunderstood me. I don't want a *church* wedding, but I do by all means want a *Christian* wedding. And I will also wear a garland and veil. I don't accept the Baptist view there. They say, "I shall wear no crown of honor here, where my Lord wore the crown of thorns." But I just don't see any connection.

Today it's very cold. We went to Hersfeld together and did some shopping. I'll either order my wedding dress, or buy it together with you. I wrote to Berlin asking the Köhlers to forward my mail here. By the way, it's strange that your brother Hermann and Käthe haven't sent me a birth announcement yet.

Take good care of your health. Do you have a good appetite? And are you getting proper food? God protect you, my dearest love. I think of you all the time.

With infinite love,
your faithful bride

Erlangen
May 15, 1909

My Emmy,

It's been a while since I wrote. I keep procrastinating because of my work: the more I get into it, the more it seems to mushroom. Tomorrow, in spite of the gloriously alluring, fresh spring weather, I'll have to stay indoors again to get off a number of letters and continue my studies. Oh well – I got up at five o'clock this morning instead and took a wonderful morning outing to Atzelsberg, where I picked a lovely little bouquet of periwinkle to send you, and to decorate your portrait in my room. It gave me new energy to continue working. In two weeks we'll be together. I'm so happy! Before then, however, there's a tremendous amount to do. Please write me in the meantime about everything you're experiencing and above all about your love, which is my greatest joy on earth. I'm extremely lonely here.

With ardent kisses,
your happy Ebbo

Bebra
May 16, 1909

Matthew 5:6: "Blessed are those who hunger and thirst for righteousness, for they will be filled."

Revelation 22:17: "The Spirit and the bride say, 'Come!' And let him who hears say, 'Come!' Whoever is thirsty, let him come; and whoever wishes, let him take the free gift of the water of life."

My Ebbo,

You can't imagine how much my soul thirsts to be more deeply immersed in God and to live solely for him. My life often seems to me so fruitless and still so full of self, even though he has promised that streams of living water shall flow from whoever believes. I *do* believe.

Incidentally, I recently received a card from Frau Baehr. Isn't that touching? Another thing: Else has been in Berlin since yesterday, and Frau Köhler invited her to the May meetings. She's also been invited to Fräulein von Patow's in Zimmitz. We need to remember her in our prayers.

I thought of arranging my upcoming trip as follows: I want to stay in Bebra when you come (though I might spend a few days in Seligenthal this week). I'll then be in Halle around June 10, stay there a few days to put my things in order, and return to Berlin after that. I'm looking forward to the 29th so much! When will you be in Eisenach?

May God protect you until then, my dearest love, and greatly bless you in your work.

With deep love and great expectation,
your Emmy

Erlangen
May 16, 1909

Acts 2:39: "The promise is for *you* and your children and for all who are far off – for all whom the Lord our God will call."

Proverbs 2:4–5: "If you look for it as for silver and search for it as for hidden treasure, then you will understand the fear of the Lord and find the knowledge of God."

Most beloved, delightful sweetheart,

Your letter today made such a deep and blessed impression on me that I simply can't help responding to it, even if briefly, above all to what you wrote about your deep thirst for a fruitful life, lived wholly and solely in God and for him. That corresponds most fully with my own longing. Emmy, as much as the Lord has given us (and we can't be grateful enough for it), I've come to the conviction that there is still much that must become completely different in both of us. Our upward flight must bear us still higher and more powerfully away from all that is earthly *to him,* so that we can be refreshed by his pure clarity and find strength for service on earth – strength that can't be gained in any other way than by being immersed in God! I feel that I am still so immature, untruthful, and affected. But I *thirst* for the pure fountain of divine truth in which all impure human admixtures have disappeared, as in the purity of crystal. Even as I write of this longing, I lack this purity, for it comes so much out of my own, unpurified self. This is why I believe we must become *completely new.* We must start *all over again* with our Christianity, lay the foundation once more, and cast off all dross from ourselves. This should be our goal when we're together in twelve days and can discuss everything of importance and bring it before God. Now, unfortunately, I have to close.

With an ardent kiss,
your faithful Ebbo

I'm getting a lot out of Proverbs and the Book of Acts, which happens when I read less, and pray and reflect more. Today I read Proverbs 2 and the second half of Acts 3.

Bebra
May 18, 1909

Beloved Ebbo,

I just received your loving letter and am sitting down straight away to tell you how very much I, too, struggle to be *completely* filled with God. Seeing so much selfishness and sin, so much worldliness and also untruthfulness, in fellow believers (and especially in myself), I've been transfixed of late with the longing to live more deeply and completely for God. Yes, Ebbo, let's use our days together well so that they can bless us like never before. I know we both want to surrender everything to him through prayer and to arrange everything in our lives in accordance with Romans 12:1–2: "Therefore, I urge you, brothers, in view of God's mercy, to offer your bodies as living sacrifices, holy and pleasing to God – this is your spiritual act of worship. Do not conform any longer to the pattern of this world, but be transformed by the renewing of your mind. Then you will be able to test and approve what God's will is – his good, pleasing and perfect will." There is so much on my heart. May I become a truly blessed witness for Jesus, like Catherine Booth, and not occupy myself merely with the trivialities of this earth, even though they have their place. In this vein, my darling, let's really not spend too much on the wedding.

In deepest love,
your Emmy

Erlangen
May 22, 1909

Beloved Emmy,

I'm so glad you're visiting your friends in Seligenthal. It must be a marvelous area.

My only darling! I believe we both need much more spiritual energy for saving the lost. We can't look at present-day Christians, who on the whole are extremely poor (and of whom I'm sure I'm one of the most wretched). Much more than that, we must seize upon the abundant promises of God and allow ourselves to be transformed and equipped by him, even if no one understands us. Powerful renewals and movements of the Spirit await us. Let us begin with ourselves – it may demand painful purification – and then work together in the strength of the Spirit.

If I were you, I'd stay in Seligenthal until the end of the week. But I absolutely must get to work now. Every fiber of my being rejoices in anticipation of our meeting.

Your forever grateful Ebbo

Over Whitsun Eberhard spent several days together with Emmy in Seligenthal, an idyllic Thuringian village where they enjoyed peace for the first time in months, and where the revival movement was currently at its height. At meetings held mostly in farmers' houses or village schools, many people found faith in Christ and made practical changes in their lives that reflected their newfound convictions.

Halle
June 14, 1909

Isaiah 28:16: "The one who trusts will never be dismayed."

My deeply beloved Ebbo,

I'm staying at the Zabelers with Else because they're redecorating at home. Frau Zabeler cares for me most touchingly, but otherwise I'm not spending much time with her family. Things are going well with Mama at the moment, but living at home won't work out in the long run. We need to pray for her conversion.

It was wonderful to talk with you on the telephone. I was so happy to hear your voice again and am looking forward inexpressibly to seeing you soon. Until then I'll keep working hard on my wedding dress. I've finished a lot of the sewing already.

There's something else I want to write about: Several things have occurred to me recently in regard to sins I committed before my conversion. I'm ready to confess to the people involved.

1) In Salzwedel I often spoke unfavorably of some sisters, out of envy.

2) At the Freybes I often took fruit out of the garden without their knowing.

3) When I withdrew from the Deaconesses' Home, I acted as if I was doing so at Papa's suggestion or request, when in fact it was my own idea to quit. There may be other things like that, which I haven't yet recognized.

Through seeing these sins for what they are, my entire lower nature has become much more obvious to me; but Jesus has become much greater to me as well. It's very hard for me to admit these things, my only beloved, but I've done it so that you can bring them before God and discern whether I need to confess them in order to be completely free and pure before him and usable for him. I praise God that I can tell you *everything*. But now I must close, my dear Ebbo. May God protect you.

Yours faithfully,
Emmy

Erlangen
June 15, 1909

Most precious Emmy,

I'm extremely happy how the Lord is bringing you further and further into the light of his spirit, you sweet little bird. God wants everything he's given us to bring forth glorious fruit and not to have been granted us in vain.

In regard to your three points:

1) You already wrote plainly to the matron at the Deaconesses' Home about envying and judging other women you worked with. That was definitely a sin, but there isn't anything else you can do about it now, except to believe that it's placed under Jesus, through whose blood all envy is washed away, and to

seek love – love alone – for all human beings. Love is, after all, the first fruit of the Spirit. See Galatians.

2) If you were in any way untruthful about how you came to step down from your position at the Home, that's very disappointing. However, I believe that if confessing a lie won't repair the damage caused by it, that particular lie should be confessed only to God. The main thing, then, is to become more radical, honest, and transparent.

3) I certainly believe that every theft, whether small or large, ought to be confessed so that restitution can be made wherever possible. Only you can know whether the matter of the Freybes' fruit falls under this, or whether you were generally allowed to take fruit from their garden, in which case helping yourself would not really count as stealing.

According to my experience, it is important

1) to be completely truthful and ready to do anything, in other words, to hate all sin.

2) not to fall outside of the grace of redemption, but to remain very peacefully in it.

3) not to search sin out in an unnatural way, where there was actually innocence.

4) to continually seek for deeper purification everywhere.

I must close now, beloved heart. I love you more and more – you have no idea how I look up to you.

Kissing you in the happiness of Jesus,
your Eberhard

Windeck
June 19, 1909

Isaiah 40:26: "Lift your eyes and look to the heavens: Who created all these? He who brings out the starry host one by one, and calls them each by name. Because of his great power and mighty strength, not one of them is missing."

My sweetest Emmy,

This morning, in a holy hour of prayer, and then again through my concentrated studies on the great atheist Feuerbach, it became more important to me than ever that, in our proclamation and in our daily lives, our main emphasis ought to be on Jesus' love to us and our love to him and to all around us – that is, on the experience of the heart!

Kissing you in this deep love,
your Ebbo

I picked these forget-me-nots for you in the woods.

Halle
July 3, 1909

Psalm 84

Ecclesiastes 3:11: "He has made everything beautiful in its time. He has also set eternity in the hearts of men; yet they cannot fathom what God has done from beginning to end."

My deeply beloved Ebbo,

Else and I will travel to Berlin on Friday, July 9, God willing. I'm looking forward to the trip very much.

You know, my Ebbo, the Bible is becoming greater and greater for me, as I recognize its truth more and more. I simply can't understand it anymore when people live only for the moment, and for themselves and their pleasure. I feel sorry for such poor, deluded people. And to think that our parents and brothers and sisters are in this situation too! We must pray that they find and accept Jesus soon.

Ebbo, you wouldn't believe how much I'm looking forward to the 26th, when we'll be together again at last. I'm constantly counting the days. Let's hope we won't need to be separated for such long periods after that. And let's pray that the Lord leads everything!

Your Emmy

Erlangen
July 5, 1909

Beloved bride,

Three weeks from today, if God wills it, I'll at last be able to look into the eyes of the most beloved and revered soul I know, a person without whom life would seem almost too heavy a burden to carry – yes, a soul I love and need above all other living beings. If only we could remain together for a long time! I'm hoping for this with my whole heart. I don't want to be at the Köhlers, however. We'll simply have to look for a better place. (By the way, I just received an invitation from the Wiegands for August 10.) In the meantime, here is what I foresee for the rest of the summer:

1) From July 26 until August 7 I'll be in or near Berlin, working in a library there, where I have a lot to do.

2) On August 9 or 11 we'll meet in Bebra, after I go to Erfurt or Weimar. Please write me whether you received the invitation and whether Else is also invited, which would be most pleasant for us.

3) My plans for September depend on where you're staying. Should you need to be in Halle again, I could move in with Gotthelf Müller and come to see you every Sunday.

What a grace it would be, if it all turned out that way! In October I'd then have to study here again, so as to get through everything as soon as possible. Unfortunately, Professor Falckenberg intends to be in Italy until the end of October, so it's doubtful that he'll find time to look through my work before November 15.

By the way, beloved Emmy, don't get your hopes too high for our time together in Berlin, and nor will I. From the end of July until October (and even more from then until the exam) I simply must place studying above everything else, if I don't want to endanger our future. So apart from Sundays, we'll see little of each other and then only for brief periods. I'm telling you this now so that you don't look at me sadly and reproachfully, or make me feel that I'm spending too little time with you, my dear, and too much with my books. That would be very hard for me, since I'll have to overcome myself as well. You do understand, don't you, my darling? I'm writing this only so that you won't be disappointed later. But for now, let me embrace you with the sheer joy I have even in contemplating the glorious, long time we'll have once we're together again, and let my exulting heart lift you high into the air. O Emmy – you are my life's happiness, my delight, my all in Jesus!

It's so wonderful how deeply the Lord is working on us both, and how just in recent days there was new proof that he intends to do something with the two of us, that he wants to educate us so that we become completely humbled people, filled with the Spirit, whom he can use for the saving of many (I long to say many thousands)! Dear Emmy, your precious letter of this morning was a great blessing to me, and I read Psalm 84 in deep dialogue with God. The main things he wants for me are 1) an awareness of sin and humbling, 2) full surrender and renunciation of the world, and 3) deep community of love with God and Jesus.

Please, Emmy, always think of these three points when you pray for me, because hidden in them lies full victory for us.

Emmy, when I pray these days, I always pray for you as if I were praying for myself. Until now I wasn't able to do that for anyone else, and not even always for you, because such prayer requires a holy heedlessness toward oneself (and thus toward one's own ego as well), which is naturally hard to attain. I have also sacrificed to the Lord, among many other things, my terrible ambition for you. I now want to praise him even if, for example, Else surpasses you in blessing and power – something I could never have done earlier. Altogether I no longer want to be zealous for you to be honored above others. Instead, I want nothing for you but one thing: that you become a woman who is infinitely blessed, full of the Holy Spirit and the power to bring forth rich fruits for him in many thousands, and best of all in such a way that people don't regard and admire it. See, Emmy, this is the way I pray for you and for myself. This is the way I beseech the Lord for a much more godly and blessed life than we ever planned for ourselves or can ever plan. Let's use every opportunity, therefore, to enter more deeply into him and become freer of people. Deepen your faith as much as you can in regard to what you wrote in your last letter: 1) the truth of the word of God and the love to seek it out, and 2) the misery and folly of men, and dedication and prayer for their salvation. In this way you'll be filled by the Holy Spirit and will become a woman like Catherine Booth, with a thousand paths of blessing and all of them reaching into eternity.

Duty calls me to close this letter, but in the meantime let's hurry with all our strength to convey his message to this dying, sinking world.

United in full dedication to Jesus, our glorious king,
your loyal Ebbo

The Home Stretch

As Eberhard prepared himself for the last and most difficult phase of his studies, Emmy returned (July 10) to Berlin to care for the Köhler children while their parents were away on vacation.

Erlangen
July 18, 1909

Best beloved Emmy,

Having just spent a holy hour with God poring over the wonderful book of Ezra, I'm writing you this letter, which will be the last longish one for a while. I've gained enormous blessings from reading Ezra; now I think we ought to read the prophets Haggai and Zechariah, because they belong with it (see Ezra 5:1–2 and 6:14), and then continue with Nehemiah and Esther. I'd still like to discuss Ezra with you because much of it hits me directly.

You'll understand me rightly, my darling, if I confess to you that in thoughts and feelings, and perhaps even more in extravagant words, I've frequently idolized you in such a way that God's honor was injured by it. Of course I love you more deeply, truly, and faithfully than ever, as much as anyone can love – to the very highest human degree – but I also want to be fully obedient to God's spirit, and love you more and more *in the spirit of him who is love.* It is for this reason – that is, out of faithfulness to him and love to you – that I henceforth want to avoid every feeling, thought, and expression that exalts or idolizes you, or puts you above other people. In other words, I want to see you, too, as a *human being,* sinful and lost without Jesus, and all-glorious and all-pure only in him.

I know these thoughts will be entirely in accordance with your own, my dear songbird, but I feel the need to express them plainly at least once, as part of my freeing from old ways. I hereby renounce all honor of my own as well, and I pray (and here you will have to help me) that from now on, everything we do will be in keeping, also practically speaking, with this resolve. But enough about that! *Life* is the real proof, through the Lord's grace. When I'm in Berlin we'll talk about our future together so that we can truly live in the spirit of Jesus, and not in the spirit of the fashionable (or even unfashionable) world. After all, our desire is to seek Jesus alone. Oh Emmy, how *much* I look forward to being with you soon!

Greet Else, and the Köhlers and Meichsners and Warns, too, please. Hermann wrote to me very warmly and also inquired about you. Käthe is not as well as she should be, but her illness doesn't seem like it will have any serious consequences.

Loving you from the depths of my heart, and happy in Jesus,

your faithful bridegroom

Shortly after arriving in Berlin, Emmy became aware that there was an unhealthy relationship, perhaps even a secret engagement, between the Köhlers' eldest daughter, fourteen-year-old Annemarie, and Johannes Warns, a thirty-five-year-old evangelist. Emmy was not the only one to be troubled: Warns was widely known in the revival movement, and his involvement with the girl had been noticed by others. As news of the scandal spread, Emmy arranged to leave Berlin as soon as possible.

Eberhard, meanwhile, had barely a moment's rest over the next weeks as he prepared for his forthcoming doctoral exam. By the end of July he had submitted his final major paper on Immanuel Kant. After this he traveled to Weimar to gather information from the Nietzsche Archives for his dissertation. Confident of success, he also began searching for suitable living quarters in Leipzig, where the young couple planned to settle, at least for the time being.

Markleeberg
September 28, 1909

Emmy,

You're the star and the happiness of my life and, through God's grace, my source of courage and strength. Without you I'd be defeated in the day-to-day struggle of life. I need you, Emmy; and how full of goodness the Lord is, that he knows this and has given you to me. It's even more glorious, though, that he has granted me complete redemption. You simply won't believe how wretched I've felt, contemplating my whole miserable being, and my dreadfully inadequate Christianity. The only comfort is that it doesn't depend on *me* at all, but on the perfect salvation found in Christ and in his word. And you're the only person on the entire planet who can tangibly prove to me the glory and love of God.

Thank you very much, by the way, for the sweet letter I found waiting for me last night in Oetzsch. Today after studying I went out into the neighborhood here, and that's where I'm writing this letter now. Yesterday I wasn't able to write because I was in Leipzig all day. I had three meetings to attend, made four house visits, and was constantly together with Dr. Pitschel. He is so loving and devoted. He strongly advised me to withdraw completely so as to concentrate on my studies in Weimar.

Pitschel and I went together to see a nice apartment, but it was already rented out. He also gave me heaps of practical advice and again invited you to stop by their house. By the way, I again noticed yesterday how harmful it is to run and chase from morning till evening. We'll need to protect each other from that sort of life in the future. At least half of every day ought to be reserved for quiet, deepening, and family fellowship, or the devil will overthrow us. O Emmy, how I *long* to set up a home with you at long last! I don't deserve such great happiness, but if the Lord wills it, it *will* happen, in just three months.

Praising him for you, my glorious little bird,
your Ebbo

Weimar
October 18, 1909

My darling, delightful, beloved bride,

If *only* the next ten weeks were already over! If only I were able to have already sent a telegram saying, "Passed! Ebbo, Ph.D!" There doesn't need to be any *magna* or *summa cum laude* attached to it. Then we'd also have received another 1000 Marks, etc., and you'd be sitting by me in your lovely wedding gown, and I'd be whispering into your sweet ear (have you ever noticed that you have *much* prettier ears than others?) about my love for you. What happiness!

My studies went forward very well today. Since our most recent conversations I have much more courage and am more assured of victory. It's true I've often wondered if I could stand living all this time without you. But that's unfair to God, who has been so faithful and kind to us. The important thing now is to take down the last barriers. And with God I can believe I *can* leap over every remaining wall, and also over the stupid exam, without falling.

O Emmy, if you only knew how beautiful your eyes were yesterday as we walked home together along the Promenade! See you soon in Weimar. May God protect you till then.

Hugs and kisses,
your Ebbo

Halle
October 26, 1909

My beloved Ebbo,

Since I wrote to you only briefly yesterday, I want to send you another greeting. Today we received a certificate (forwarded from Berlin-Schöneberg), confirming Else's and my withdrawal from the state church and requiring us to make a withdrawal payment of six Marks, sixty Pfennig. Imagine Mama's horror! At first she refused to accept it from the postman, but of course that wasn't possible, so she ended up having to receive it and even pay for it! I had to pay her back, however, also for Else.

How are your studies going? Will you finish the copying this week? Be careful that it doesn't become too much for you. It would be much better to let it take a couple of days longer than planned, than have it affect your health. Anyway, I don't see how you can possibly finish everything by Christmas. Besides, my parents want to be forewarned at least one month in advance of our wedding. So don't wear yourself out – also because if you do, you won't have enough energy to prepare for the oral exam. God willing, we'll have a beautiful Christmas together no matter what, and it really won't be so bad if we have to wait a bit longer for the wedding.

Please let me know when you're going to Erlangen, so that I can pray for you, especially that the Lord protects you! And don't take the D-train so often. It scares me! I keep wondering when you'll come. First you said Tuesday, then Thursday, and now Saturday. Well, even if you can't make it on Saturday, you really must come by Sunday.

Your loving, loyal Emmy

Weimar
October 26, 1909

Sweetest Emmy,

I can't stand not being able to talk with you any longer! Can you do me a big favor and be at the telephone at 12:15? If that won't work, please telegraph me and let me know what time is good for you. O Emmy, I have such a longing to be with you, and yet I'm the one holding up the wedding because of my work. It's terrible. But what more can I do? Even working without interruptions and writing almost the whole day, I still doubt I'll be able to travel on Friday, though I do still hope to make it to Erlangen on Saturday.

Please don't worry, though. I really believe the Lord will give me my degree by December 15. Just pray hard for me, my little bird, that I don't get too upset about the delay.

Until then, I'd better get back to work. I'm counting on talking to you tomorrow noon.

Your Ebbo

Halle
October 27, 1909

My deeply beloved Ebbo,

When I got your sweet letter this morning, I was at first deeply disappointed, but now I think it would be much better to postpone the wedding after all, than for you to get overworked. So stop cramming – especially if you're not going to finish everything by Christmas anyway. It's not so terrible. Take the time you need, and please go for an hour's walk every day, and don't work later than 9:30. That's late enough. Can't you skip going to Erfurt just this once, and also Halle next Sunday? You can still go to Erlangen at the beginning of next week if necessary. I just don't like it that you travel so far so often. As a matter of fact, why do you have to go there if you're no longer worried about the date of our wedding? Or are you? Please, *please* don't wear yourself out, and take care of yourself. If you get sick, I simply won't know what to do.

Please make sure you have someone send your winter overcoat. And are you taking Somatose three times a day? You have to be strong for the oral exam.

In suspense, but with my deepest love,
your bride

Weimar
October 27, 1909

Best beloved songbird,

I was very sad after our call today because I sensed that you're worried about me and generally distressed. I went back to work with more determination than ever, and the Lord heard my deep sighs. I managed a sizable amount of work and copied thirty-one columns. (As I think I told you, there's no extra work at this point, as there was earlier.)

Here's an outline of what I still need to accomplish: There's a total of sixty-one and a half pages to be copied, but I've completed forty-three, so I have only eighteen and a half more to do. I want to revise a few things and look them up in the concordance, so I need the next three days, until Saturday. But I think I can promise you that I'll be finished by then without getting overworked.

My dissertation will be somewhat shorter than I thought. I cut down the first part as much as I could since it was much too long, and now it will probably come out to one hundred and ten pages. Of these, seventy-nine are finished, leaving me with about thirty more pages of the draft still to copy. I'll then need about four weeks to prepare for the oral, so that when Falckenberg gives me the go-ahead, the exam can be scheduled, either at the end of November or in the very first days of December.

But Emmy, dear Emmy! You *can't* let yourself become discouraged now, just when we have more reason than ever to be joyful. You don't need to be in the least worried about my health. As you know, work always agrees just fine with me. It's nervous excitement that does me in. So please be cheerful and full of trust. Above all, believe that the Lord will lead us from victory to victory.

Considerate of all your wishes, but wanting to be sensible too, and sending you many kisses,

your loyal Ebbo, who lives for you

As Eberhard's final examination loomed, Emmy's parents grew increasingly incensed over his "irresponsible neglect" of his studies. They reproached him for running himself ragged giving talks and holding meetings instead of focusing single-mindedly on preparing for a day that would be so crucial for his and Emmy's future. As if that wasn't enough, he had rented a tiny, four-room apartment in Leipzig for him and Emmy to occupy in January, a move they condemned as premature.

Weimar
November 15, 1909

My dear, sweet Emmy,

I just received a letter from Professor Falckenberg. He writes, "I have gone through your thesis. Reading it gave me real pleasure, and I congratulate you on the successful outcome of your work. My wife is also happy that I can give you such gratifying information. Now go outdoors and take frequent walks, so that you have energy for the oral examination. Best wishes and a joyful *auf Wiedersehen,* Dr. R. Falckenberg."

Isn't that tremendous, my little bride? And isn't it a sign that Jesus is with us again, right after I have purified myself for him? Let's not be of little faith in anything now! (By the way, fifty Marks just came in from von Gerdtell, too.)

As you can imagine, I'm returning to my work with new vigor now – and there is in fact a huge amount facing me. Falckenberg says the week from the 29th to the 4th may be open for the oral, but he can't say definitely yet, as it depends on the dean. Still, Emmy, I believe that we can (trusting in the Lord) definitely expect to celebrate our wedding around the 20th of December. Hallelujah! Hallelujah! Hallelujah!

I'm completely happy, from inside out, and full of love for you.

Always yours in Jesus, Ebbo

Pray constantly and rely completely on the Lord! I'll give you a brief update every day. And I always rejoice in the picture of you wearing that charming fur hat. It makes you look so beautiful!

Weimar
November 26, 1909

Dear, sweet Emmy,

It's just too much, to have to concentrate every ounce of strength on my philosophy studies and simultaneously be exhausted and agitated by so many obstacles. As a consequence, I'm feeling quite nervous today, also because there hasn't been any letter from you to set me at ease. It would be terrible if my great exertions were in vain, and if we had to postpone our wedding because of stupid legal papers.

As things stand, the situation is so unclear – I really don't have any idea what's going on – that there's nothing I can tell you other than the date and time of the examination: Tuesday, November 30, at six in the evening. With formalities, everything will take about two hours, so I should be able to send you a telegram shortly after eight, and you ought to receive it by ten or ten-thirty.

I'm already leaving for Erlangen tomorrow, Sunday, so send your letters on Monday and Tuesday to the Walfisch Hotel. If, by the Lord's grace, he allows me to pass the exam I will, if I can get away, travel to Halle on Tuesday night (second class, so I can sleep), arriving there at 6:30 in the morning and getting to *you* by seven o'clock, the only (apart from Jesus) glorious point of light in it all. Immediately after my arrival on Wednesday morning, I want to go to the registry office with you so that, if at all possible, we can marry on the 18th. Everything depends on having the following documents ready by Wednesday morning:

1. Our birth or baptismal certificates.
2. Our certificates of residence. A notice of removal is not adequate – it must be a certificate like the one I'm enclosing, which you must save.
3. Your certificate of domicile. This is the greatest worry since it seems to be completely out of order (and one week's prior notice is required).

Dear Emmy, pray hard that I calm down and collect myself thoroughly for the exam. I'm terribly worried that there'll be a scene at your house, or that things will somehow be spoiled because I failed in some way. I can't write any more today.

In the train en route from Weimar to Jena
November 27, 1909

As you see, I'm already on my way. My trunk has been sent ahead to Erlangen; I'm traveling third class. I'm already much calmer today: 1) because of the Lord's help yesterday evening, and 2) because of your sweet letter, which came this morning. I'm ruing the fact that I got so upset in my haste to get through everything and not imperil the wedding. I had felt that while preparing for the exam, I ought to distance myself from every source of excitement – and because of this I regrettably grew dissatisfied with you, worrying that you weren't getting your papers in order. The main guilt is in *me,* however: my lack of purity and my irritability because I couldn't cope with everything. Seeing this humbles me deeply, and I beseech you to forgive me, my dear good Emmy, who stands so high above me. But now, after everything that went so horribly wrong, I at last have certainty from the Lord (whereas before I had only hope) that I have been freed and purified. Jesus is once more everything to me, and everything is in his hands. That is my peace.

Loving you endlessly in Jesus alone,
your once-again saved Ebbo

Erlangen
November 29, 1909

Emmy, my one and only sweetheart,

Warm thanks, my darling, for the marvelous bible passages you sent. I've been reading them and praying as I do. I hope you'll send more tomorrow, too.

I hope your cold is better by Wednesday, so you can be with me – so don't go out today. This weather isn't good for your health. I am well. I pray a lot, don't work excessively, have a glass of Bordeaux wine now and then, and am eating well.

Incidentally, a very diligent, clean, twenty-three-year-old maid has been recommended to us through the Lord. She's hoping to start on January 1. She's converted and has good references, both from believers and unbelievers. I'll tell you more about her when I see you next.

Emmy, my sweet, when I'm with you again at last, from Wednesday on, we will above all things pray often and urgently and read the Bible together. I must dedicate myself all over again from the beginning. I'm determined to become more decisive and purified and stronger.

Your bridegroom, who is close to you in Jesus,
Eberhard Arnold, cand. phil.

God willing, this is the last time I'll write as a non-Ph.D.

Eberhard refused to let preparations for his examination and wedding slow him down. On the evening before his oral, he gave a lecture near Weimar. Following it, he hired a horse-drawn sleigh to take him to the train station and then traveled all night, arriving in Erlangen by morning. The examination was set to begin at six that evening. Shortly after eight, Emmy received a telegram:

Telegraphie des Deutschen Reiches.

Halle (Saale).

November 30, 1909

Dispatched from Erlangen	To Emmy von Hollander
7:35 PM	Dessauerstrasse 8a
	8:17 PM

Summa cum laude. Doctor of Philosophy. Ebbo.

When on Wednesday, December 1, 1909, Eberhard finally arrived in Halle and entered the von Hollander home, Dessauer Strasse 8a, it had been more than a year since he had crossed their threshold. All the same, he was welcomed as though there had never been anything between him and Emmy and her parents. They were admittedly astonished when the young man requested Emmy's papers, but Herr von Hollander was a man of his word, and after a long hesitation, he unlocked his chest and handed over the requisite documents for marriage. Two hours later, the young couple was at the registrar's office, setting their wedding day for December 20, the earliest possible date.

The long-awaited ceremony was a simple one, performed at the von Hollander house by the bride's father. When it was time for the traditional blessing, Eberhard's father stepped forward: "As you have scorned the blessing of the church, I can only give you the blessing of both parents."

Otto Mau, a family friend from Erfurt, gave a short sermon. His text was "Jesus sent out his disciples two by two," from Mark 6:7, and he spoke of how Eberhard and Emmy had been called by their Master together and were now being sent out into the world together, too, to serve him side by side. Ernst Klein, Eberhard's uncle, then spoke of the groom's awakening and conversion as a teen, and of how he had been guided and led by his faith ever since then – and wished for the same in the future.

Then it was off to the reception at the Crown Prince Hotel, and after that, a cab to the train station where the young couple boarded an express to Leipzig. "After almost three years," Emmy later wrote, "we felt as free as birds in the air."

Epilogue

From 1910 to 1915, the Arnolds moved from one city to another, mostly on account of Eberhard's work as a public speaker and officer for various Christian organizations, including the YMCA. Addressing large audiences on a variety of religious questions, he was often away from home several nights a week. Emmy, meanwhile, was busy with a growing family that eventually included five children.

During the difficult years of the first World War (1914–18), the pressing social, economic, and political issues of the day led the couple to read the Bible with new eyes. Their searching soon carried them far beyond what they had experienced during the awakening in Halle. In Eberhard's words, the time demanded a discipleship that "transcended merely edifying experiences." Writing in 1931, Emmy summarized the shift:

> As deeply as the message of the revival in Halle had penetrated our hearts – that Christ died for each sinner and that through his death each individual is redeemed – another message reached us just as forcibly in our searching: God wants to rule not only the lives of individuals but the whole

world – the world of economic, social, and political structures. And we were struck by the fact that God doesn't govern the so-called Christian world; Satan does.

Social contradictions such as the fact that one person can enjoy the plenty of life without sweating, while another does not have bread for his children, despite working like a slave, occupied us more and more. Through reading the Bible, especially the prophets, the Sermon on the Mount, and the Letter of James, we realized that this is not God's will.

From the outset of our friendship, Eberhard and I had wanted to give our lives in service to others. It was in this sense that we were engaged. Already then, it was the proclamation of the gospel and service to humankind that was our primary concern, not our personal lives and relationships. So it was perhaps natural that we now found ourselves joining with people who were dissatisfied and were challenging public life and human relationships with the old slogans of freedom, equality, and fraternity. These ideals were drawing people from everywhere: members of the youth movement, anarchists, socialists, communists, reformers, artists, Free Germans, former army officers, and even some pietists. All of them were struggling to find God's will, even if not all of them would have expressed it like that. One issue that particularly stirred us in a series of open evenings at our house in 1919 was our common guilt. We felt that we were responsible not only for our personal lives, but also for the condition of today's world.

There was a cry in these circles for someone to show the way out of the confusion. The war had shaken many people's childlike faith in God. Some could no longer believe in a God of love. Many were confused by the churches, since pastors on both sides had blessed weapons, hurried soldiers onto fields of slaughter, and prayed for the victory of their own nation.

The enslavement of the proletariat was also a burning question. Why should millions of miners have to risk life and limb to dig coal, while the directors who ran the mines lived in luxury on large country estates? Before long we were reaching out to poor families and individuals in northern and western Berlin who lived in terrible circumstances. We saw people living seven in one room, or crowded in damp cellars without windows. But we also saw how little was achieved by means of social reform...

At our open evenings we read the Sermon on the Mount and were so overwhelmed by it that we decided to rearrange our lives completely, cost what it may. Everything written there seemed to have been spoken directly to us: from the Beatitudes to what Jesus says about justice, about hungering for righteousness, loving one's enemies, praying, seeking God's kingdom first, and finally doing God's will. The Sermon on the Mount was also being illuminated for us from other sides. We discovered the message of the Blumhardts, Francis of Assisi, the early Quaker George Fox, the Jewish thinkers Martin Buber and Gustav Landauer, and others.

Our friends from the SCM and other fellowship Christians didn't understand how we could mingle with the sort of people I have mentioned in order to seek with them.

They were concerned solely with bringing the sins of the individual in order before God, and couldn't understand why we took up "social" and "political" questions. But we felt we had to sit on the same bench with those who had not yet experienced the grace of God in their personal lives. We believed Jesus when he said, "Everyone on the side of truth listens to me" (John 18:37), and the words in Proverbs 2:7: "He holds victory in store for the upright." Here our faith was rock-firm: that every seeker after truth would somehow find the way to Truth. But we were pretty much alone in this.

In early March 1920 Eberhard decided to give notice at *Die Furche,* the Christian publishing house where he had worked since 1915. The view there was that we should be preaching the grace of God without mixing in other things. It wasn't easy because we loved the people, but the constant disagreements and tensions were unproductive.

Just around this time Eberhard was asked to take over the *Neuwerk* Publishing House, a new venture of the Free German Youth. *Neuwerk* was more than a business – it was a movement of young people who shared our ideals and intentions to live according to the Gospels, perhaps in an intentional community or rural settlement.

Emmy also remembered Eberhard saying one day during this time of upheaval, "I can no longer speak and hold lectures – at least not until I change my life to what Jesus wants it to be." He had been struck by a sentence from the *Didache,* an early

Christian text he had studied, which says, "By his standard of living will both the false prophet and the true be recognized." To quote Eberhard directly, from an address he gave in 1933:

> In my youth, I tried to lead people to Jesus through studying the Bible, and through talks and discussions. But there came a time when I recognized that this was no longer enough. I began to see the tremendous power of mammon, of discord, of hate, and of the sword: the hard boot of the oppressor upon the neck of the oppressed. I saw that dedication to the soul alone did not fulfill all of Jesus' commandments; he wanted us to care for men's bodies as well.
>
> From 1913 to 1917 Emmy and I sought painfully for an understanding of the truth. Shortly before the outbreak of the war, I had written to a friend saying that I could not go on. I had preached the gospel, but felt that I needed to do more. Gradually it became clear to us that the way of Jesus was practical and tangible. It was more than concern for the soul. He said, very simply: "If you have two coats, give to him who has none. Give food to the hungry, and do not turn away from your neighbor when he needs you. When asked for an hour's work, give two. Strive for justice. If you want to marry and start a family, then see that those around you can do the same. If you seek education and work, make these available to others also. And if it is your duty to care for your own health, then fulfill this duty to others. Treat them as you would treat yourself. Enter through the narrow gate, for it is the only way to the kingdom of God."

> We knew that we had to become as poor as beggars – that we, like Jesus, had to take upon ourselves the whole need of all people. We had to hunger for justice more than for water and bread. We knew we would be persecuted for the sake of this justice, but our righteousness would be greater than that of the moralists and theologians. And we would be filled with fire from above: we would receive the Holy Spirit. But we could not endure the life that we were living any longer.

On Midsummer's Day, 1920, the Arnolds made the plunge. Surrendering their life insurance policy for cash and leaving cosmopolitan Berlin for Sannerz, a tiny farming village (and center of the *Neuwerk* movement), they began living in full community with others. The fledgling commune grew by twists and turns. Idealists flocked to it, but most left after a short time, dissatisfied with its imperfections. To Eberhard and Emmy, however, it was never an experimental lifestyle – it was the answer to a deeply-felt calling. In Eberhard's words, "The new redemption Jesus promised is intended for us. His will is to be realized *here on earth!*"

Given the gulf between the world in which the Arnolds had been married – the grand parlors of Halle, Leipzig, and Berlin – and their new world in the youth hostels and hills of rural Hesse, it is not surprising that many of their acquaintances misunderstood them. Even close friends such as Herr von Sallwürk censured Eberhard's "fanaticism," and his sister Hannah worried that he had forsaken the centrality of Jesus in favor of some humanistic ideal, a charge that he vehemently denied.

In later years, members of the Bruderhof (as Sannerz became known) similarly misread Eberhard and Emmy's path as one that had taken them away from the Christ-centeredness of the Halle revival. In fact, their correspondence lay locked away in the community's archives for decades; and Eberhard's poems, though appreciated by a few, were derided by others for their "emotionalism." To anyone truly familiar with his voluminous writings (including his very last letters and poems, from the fall of 1935) it is clear that neither he nor Emmy ever wavered in the slightest from the fervor of their youth, and from their insistence that without a personal relationship to Jesus, the most noble "Christian" endeavor in the world will falter and fail. To quote from a letter Eberhard wrote to his sister Hannah in March 1925:

> My long years of work building up the fellowship movement and evangelizing have always been an essential part of my life. It is a totally false report if you have been told that I ever rejected the revival movement or its Christianity. I have never expressed disapproval in the sense that the forgiveness of sins was being too strongly placed in the foreground. On the contrary, I am convinced that it is impossible to overemphasize the forgiveness of sins.
>
> What I do oppose energetically is when – in spite of the experience of forgiveness – someone looks away from God's great heart and gets enmeshed in his own small heart, is

completely lost in his little personal self-life, precisely in the religious sphere. An egotistical striving for personal purity, goodness, and happiness is then placed in the center of his religious experience. Even work done for others is then done with an eye to his own happiness. No wonder that even faithful members of the fellowship movement now call it old and tired! The cause of this tiredness is the false subjectivity of the self-centered life by which people devote themselves to their own little ego, or that of their neighbor.

The true destiny of the church is to fulfill God's future. That calling must become so great in our lives that we ourselves, including our private religious life, become small.

We all love the third chapter of John's Gospel, but we tend to forget that the context in which personal rebirth is placed there is the supra-personal context of God's kingdom. I question a rebirth that has no connection with God's coming kingdom, and I believe that God awakens many who open themselves to this kingdom but are still unclear about their personal forgiveness and salvation.

We need to be given the strength to testify to the new birth from the Holy Spirit to those who are in this process of awakening. That was what Jesus did to Nicodemus, a man who was gripped by the kingdom. But it is just as important to give Christians a clear and definite witness about their great responsibility in respect to social justice, in respect to Christ's coming reign of peace, and therefore in respect to the demands and promises of his Sermon on the Mount.

To recount the course of Eberhard and Emmy's subsequent lives would take too much space here. Eberhard died in 1935, after a long and difficult surgery. Two years later, the community that had gathered around him was expelled from the country by Hitler's National Socialist government. Emmy lived on for several more decades, witnessing the flowering of her husband's vision as it took shape in numerous daughter communities in Europe, South America, and the northeastern United States. She died in upstate New York in 1980, at the age of ninety-five.

Neither Eberhard nor Emmy would have wanted to be memorialized, either as founders of a movement or by books such as this one. What they gave their lives for has far greater significance than any human legacy. In Emmy's words:

> It is quite clear that nobody can live off memories from the past. Today, too, the Spirit lives, calling people as in the time of John the Baptist: "Repent, for the kingdom of heaven is at hand!" Jesus still calls men and women to follow him, to leave everything in search of the one precious pearl. Here and there this is happening now.

For Further Reading

Arnold, Eberhard. *Selected Writings*
A modest but comprehensive collection covering a wide range of topics, and the best book by which to become familiar with Arnold's faith.

Arnold, Eberhard. *The Early Christians in Their Own Words*
A classic anthology of writings from the pre-institutional, persecuted church.

Arnold, Eberhard. *Eberhard Arnold: A Testimony*
An appreciation by people who knew him, along with a small selection of letters, poems, essays, and photographs.

Arnold, Eberhard. *God's Revolution*
A collection of short excerpts from addresses, letters, and essays, topically arranged, and prefaced by a thorough profile of Arnold by the historian John Howard Yoder.

Arnold, Eberhard. *The Individual and World Need*
A hard-hitting (and still timely) look at the problem of social guilt and the question of redemption in a fallen world.

Arnold, Eberhard. *Innerland: A Guide into the Heart of the Gospel*
A voyage into the realm of the conscience and the "inner land of the invisible."

Arnold, Eberhard. *Love and Marriage in the Spirit*
Selected writings and talks on love, courtship, and marriage.

Arnold, Eberhard. *Salt and Light: Living the Sermon on the Mount*
Thoughts on the "hard teachings" of Jesus and their applicability today.

Arnold, Eberhard. *Why We Live in Community*

If selfish individualism is the problem of our time, perhaps community is the answer.

Arnold, Eberhard and Emmy. *Poems and Rhymed Prayers*

A bilingual anthology, with the German originals and English translations set side by side.

Arnold, Emmy. *A Joyful Pilgrimage: My Life in Community*

A remarkable journey from middle-class society to radical commune.

Baum, Markus. *Against the Wind: Eberhard Arnold and the Bruderhof*

The only full-length biography of Arnold, this book doubles as a history of the community movement he inspired.

Mommsen, Peter. *Homage to a Broken Man*

The dramatic life story of Heinrich Arnold, covering the history (up to 1980) of the community Eberhard and Emmy founded.

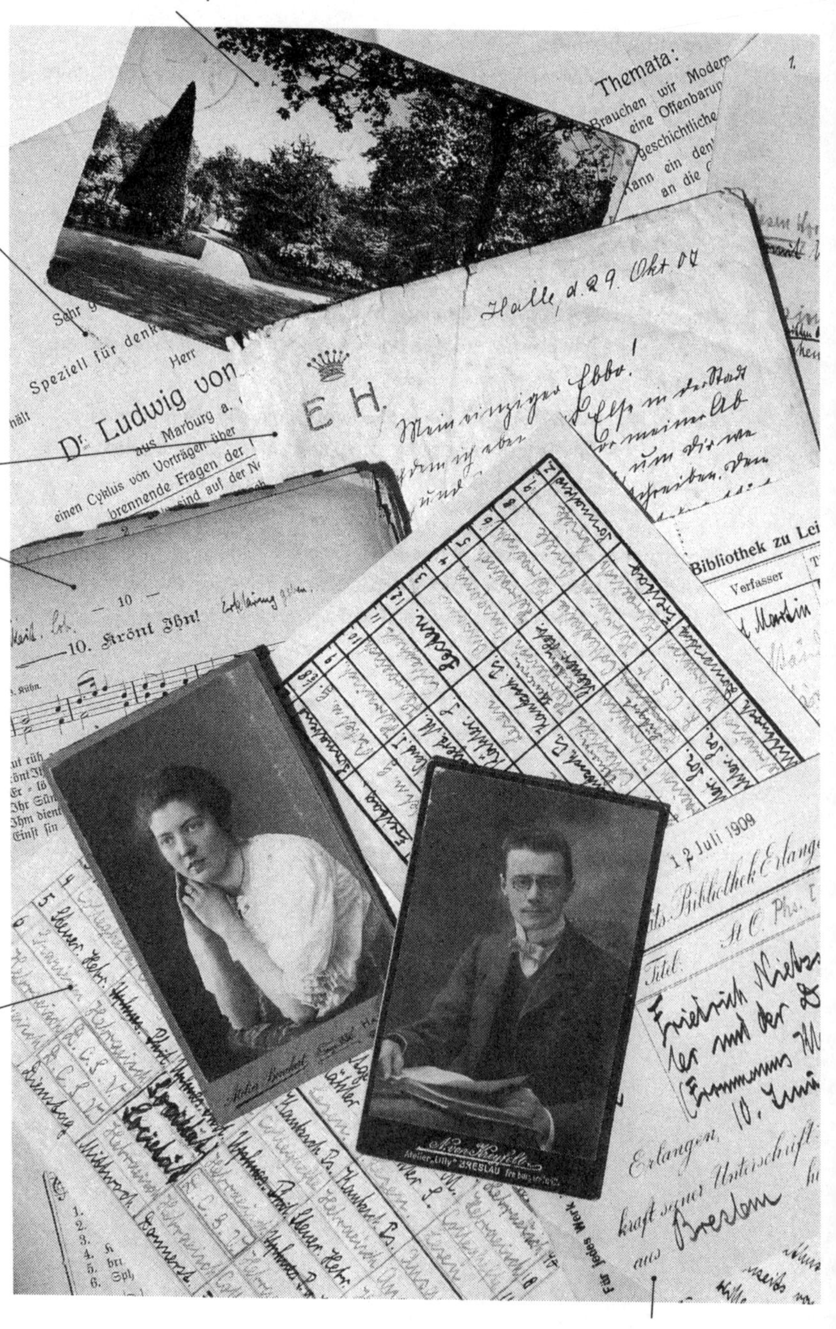

Postcard from Eberhard to Emmy

Announcement of a lecture series by Ludwig von Gerdtell

Emmy to Eberhard on von Hollander letterhead

Emmy's songbook from Halle revival days, with penned notes by Eberhard

Eberhard's class schedule for University, probably 1906

Library slip for a volume on Nietzsche from Erlangen University, dated June 1909

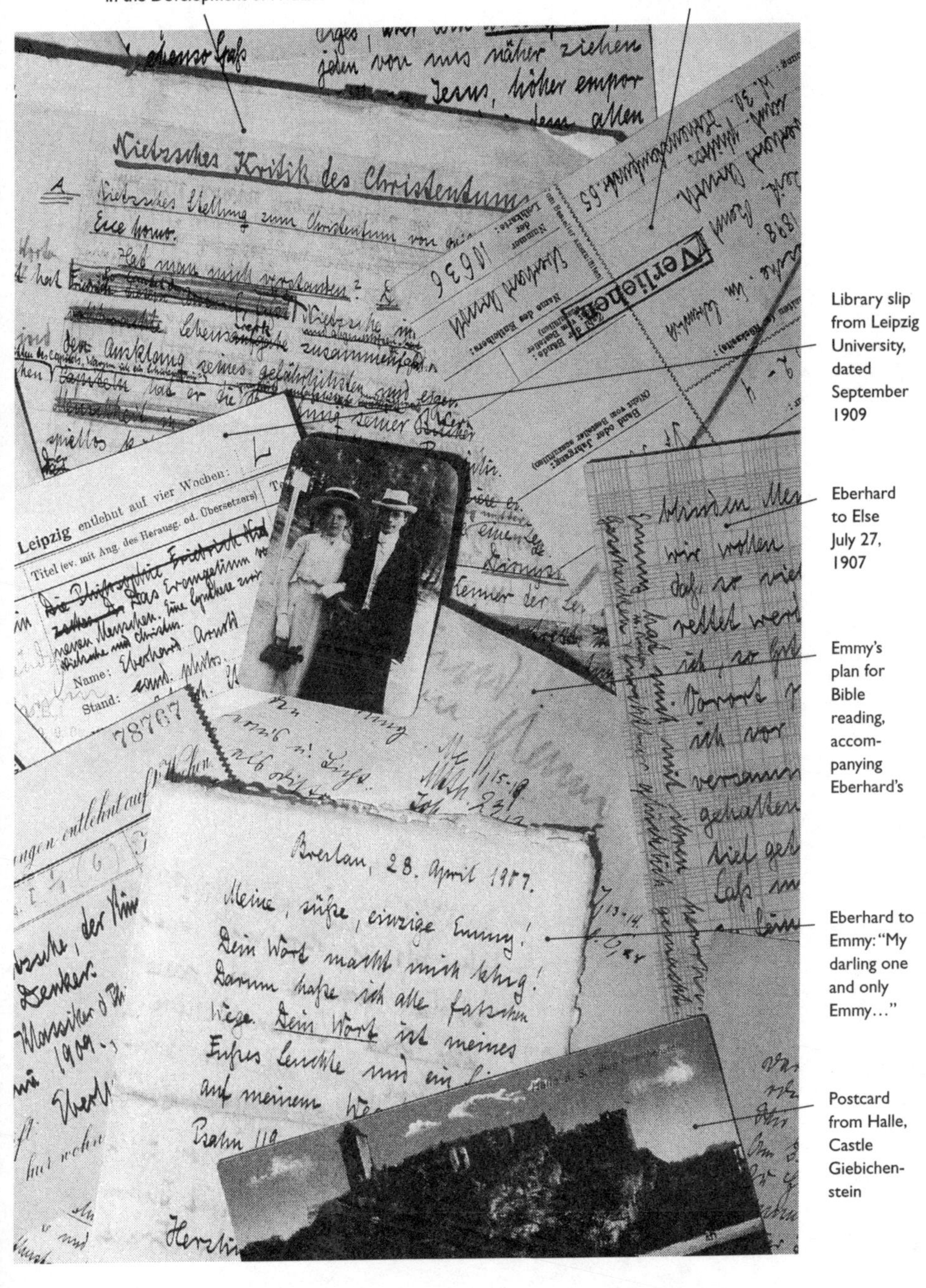

Early draft of Eberhard's doctoral thesis: "Early Christian and Anti-Christian Elements in the Development of Friedrich Nietzsche"

Library slip for a volume on Nietzsche from University of Berlin, dated August 1909

Library slip from Leipzig University, dated September 1909

Eberhard to Else July 27, 1907

Emmy's plan for Bible reading, accompanying Eberhard's

Eberhard to Emmy: "My darling one and only Emmy…"

Postcard from Halle, Castle Giebichenstein

Contact Information

Woodcrest
2032 Route 213
Rifton, NY 12471
Tel: 845-658-8351

www.plough.com

Darvell
Brightling Road
Robertsbridge, East Sussex
TN32 5DR UK
Tel: 0800 018 0799 or 44 (0)1580 88 33 44

www.ploughbooks.co.uk